Florence in the Age of the Medici and Savonarola, 1464–1498

A Short History with Documents

D1636505

Florence in the Age of the Medici and Savonarola, 1464–1498

A Short History with Documents

Kenneth Bartlett

Hackett Publishing Company, Inc.
Indianapolis/Cambridge

For further information, please address
    Hackett Publishing Company, Inc.
    P.O. Box 44937
    Indianapolis, Indiana 46244-0937

    www.hackettpublishing.com

Though every reasonable effort has been made to contact the owners of the copyrighted materials included in this book, in some instances this has proven impossible. Hackett Publishing will be glad to receive information leading to a more complete understanding of the permissions required for this book and in the meantime extends its apologies for any omissions.

Cover design by Rick Todhunter
Interior design by Laura Clark
Composition by Aptara, Inc.

Library of Congress Cataloging-in-Publication Data

Title: Florence in the age of the Medici and Savonarola, 1464–1498 : a short
    history with documents / Kenneth Bartlett.
Description: Indianapolis : Hackett Publishing Company, Inc., 2018. | Series:
    Passages: Key Moments in History | Includes bibliographical
    references and index.
Identifiers: LCCN 2017038055| ISBN 9781624666810 (pbk.) |
    ISBN 9781624666827 (cloth)
Subjects: LCSH: Florence (Italy)—History—15th century. | Florence
    (Italy)—History—15th century—Historiography.
Classification: LCC DG737.55 .F585 2018 | DDC 945/.51105—dc23
LC record available at https://lccn.loc.gov/2017038055

The paper used in this publication meets the minimum requirements of American National Standard for Information Sciences—Permanence of Paper for Printed Library Materials, ANSI Z39.48–1984.

∞

There were in Lorenzo [de'Medici] many and most excellent virtues; there were also in him some vices, due partly to nature, partly to necessity. He possessed such great authority that one could say that in his time the city was not free although it abounded in all the glory and felicity that a city can have; free in name, but in fact and in truth tyrannized over by one of its citizens. His deeds, although they can be censured in part, were very great nonetheless. . . .

And his [Savonarola's] deeds were so good in effect and some of his predictions so well borne out that many have for a long time believed that he was in truth sent by God and that he was a prophet, notwithstanding his excommunication, trial, and death. I am in doubt about it, and I have not made up my mind in any respect; and I reserve judgment, if I live that long, until the time when all will be made clear. But I am certain of this, that if he was good, we have seen in our times a great prophet; if he was bad, still a very great man, because, in addition to his learning, if he knew how to act such a great role for so many years, and so publicly, without ever being discovered in a single imposture, one must confess that he possessed a most profound judgment, and talent, and power of invention.[1]

1. Francesco Guicciardini, *The History of Florence*, quoted in J. B. Ross and M. M. McLaughlin, *The Portable Renaissance Reader* (Harmondsworth: Penguin, 1968), 267–78, 644–52.

ACKNOWLEDGMENTS

The genesis of this book belongs to my editor, Rick Todhunter of Hackett Publishing Company, who convinced me that I should contribute to the *Passages: Key Moments in History* series with a volume on Florence during the age of the Medici and Savonarola. I was happy to do so because I agreed that these years were indeed a turning point in the Florentine Renaissance and deserved a deeper analysis, illustrated by primary source texts that reflected the complexity, ambiguity, and tensions of that age. My sympathy with this approach to Florence in the *Quattrocento* was reinforced by a quarter century of teaching the senior seminar in the Renaissance Studies Program at Victoria College on Fifteenth Century Florence. Many of the themes and ideas in this book developed from my years of dialogue with the gifted and articulate students in that class. It is, consequently, to those many students over so many years that this book is in part dedicated.

My college, Victoria, in the University of Toronto, is where the Renaissance Studies Program is housed and where it arose. No flights of humanist rhetoric could in truth describe the support that Victoria has afforded me in my research and teaching career. The luxury of creating courses on the Renaissance and devising Renaissance modules for other college offerings, such as the Program in Material Culture, has been a source of continuous wonder. The freedom and flexibility to teach original, interdisciplinary classes at all levels have made my long career at Victoria one of great intellectual reward and personal satisfaction. For this book, Victoria awarded me a research grant to hire a graduate student to help discover lesser-known or more apposite original texts to illustrate my narrative. Not only did this make my work easier, it gave me the satisfaction of engaging in research with two remarkable young scholars, who were also appointed as teaching assistants in my Renaissance Culture course.

Leah Faibisoff began as the research assistant in this project and, with her exemplary knowledge of Latin and Italian, discovered some fascinating material before she left Toronto to pursue her career elsewhere. She was succeeded by Kirsty Schut, who completed the project in her professional and tireless manner, turning a long list of potential readings into a tight, coherent collection, which includes some original translations and imaginative additions. I am greatly in debt to both of these talented and energetic young scholars and thank Kirsty in particular for working to my schedule and helping so significantly to bring the selection of primary source readings to a successful conclusion. Despite the help of so many others in producing this book, any mistakes or omissions remain mine alone.

Finally, as always, I want to acknowledge the constant and loving support of my wife, Gillian, without whom nothing would ever get done, and whose brilliant editorial eye and commitment to clarity and correct syntax have been an inspiration and encouragement in my own writing. It is to her that this book is also dedicated.

My greatest hope is that this book will prove useful by stimulating students and scholars to continue to engage with the world of the Medici and Savonarola, debating the significance of this remarkable moment in Florentine history, offering different interpretations and drawing other conclusions that will carry our knowledge and understanding forward into yet another generation.

Kenneth Bartlett
Victoria College
University of Toronto

CONTENTS

Contents   xi

LIST OF ILLUSTRATIONS

PREFACE

Key Moments in the History of Florence under the Medici and Savonarola

The purpose of this book is to trace the development of one city, Florence, during a relatively brief period of its history to understand its significance not only for its own time but also for ours. Florence was in some ways just another independent republican commune in Italy, one among many. But it has always played a significant role in our contemporary interpretation of how European culture, society, and politics changed from an essentially medieval view—in which governments strove to justify the ways of God to man and to build a society that reflected that divine plan—to a new form of community in which individuals worked together to improve the condition of men and women on earth through secular means. This search for the beginnings of the "modern" concept of the self-fashioned, confident, secular individual, enlightened by ancient wisdom, and polished through mercantile and political practice, raised Florence almost to the level of an experiment in human achievement and the inception of modern concepts of the state and the individual. And there is much to recommend this idea, even if it has been challenged often by those who correctly note that change tends to be more organic and that Florence retained a great many elements of its medieval traditions, and that the Middle Ages themselves were hardly as dark and "Gothic" as Renaissance Florentine writers declared. Thus, Florence under the Medici and Savonarola legitimately represents a Turning Point in History.

What matters to us is the ability to see how individual men, families, and groups worked to achieve political goals in the context of a republican commune in which power was in theory widely distributed among the political class, that is, adult males who matriculated in a guild, owned property, and were not in arrears of taxes: about 3,000 men out of a population of no more than 50,000. We have recorded the role of faction, class, wealth, and family in driving the political discourse; and we have traced the failures of the republic, including its resorting to foreign *signori* to solve serious problems. And the successes—the creation of the Monte, and the resilience of the republic's institutions to withstand crises, such as the financial collapse and Black Death of the 1340s, the Ciompi Revolt, and Albizzi Oligarchy—are remarkable. Florence in those years did not fall into despotism, as did so many other Italian communes, but sustained a robust political culture.

But hovering over all of these considerations are the Medici. Was this family and its adherents merely another faction that controlled the republic, a loss of liberty made palatable by maintaining the outward signs of a free commune, or did the clever and moderate policies of Cosimo de'Medici provide the stability and coherence necessary for the city to prosper in peace? Did, then, the Medici destroy or guarantee the liberty of the city under Cosimo? Subsequently, Cosimo's son and grandson sustained the family's power but also changed the nature of Medici rule until Lorenzo the Magnificent became in reality an uncrowned prince.

But what do we make of their collapse and expulsion under Piero? He, like his grandfather to a lesser degree, illustrated the weaknesses of monarchy: too much depended on the ability of a successor by blood to confront the challenges of his times. The situation in Europe, Italy, and Florence was such that Piero was unable to navigate a way that would allow him to maintain Medici rule. This, too, was a Turning Point, this fall of the Medici in 1494. And the rise of Savonarola, which antedated the exile of Piero by several years, illustrates the truth that historical development is not linear, and that the causes of change are never simple.

Savonarola can be seen as a resurgence of a vigorous republicanism, animated by traditional Christian piety and the vocabulary of prophecy and divine destiny. Was this a return to medieval values, this conversion of Florence into a theocracy, in the form of a broadly participatory republic? Or was it an example of a less than peaceful transmission of power from a privileged, distant elite, alienated from their fellow citizens, to another kind of faction, with deep roots in the traditional values of the community and anxious to extend access to power to as many citizens as possible? The rise and hegemony of Savonarola were, therefore, another Turning Point in our narrative.

Finally, the fall and execution of Savonarola and the return of a more secular but still *governo largo* administration was perhaps less of a Turning Point than a recalibration of what went before, as many of the institutions that had arisen under the Dominican remained, but without his guidance; in short, then, this was more a factional transition than a Turning Point.

The principle of Key Moments in History, therefore, animates the story of Florence under the Medici and Savonarola. It is a useful vehicle for the analysis of historical change, even in so short a period, a mere sixty-four years. It also permits us to look to Florence for the roots and antecedents of modernity, cultural expression, and popular government in those years and thereby stimulate a comparison with other places at other times.

Figure 1. The Catena Map of Florence, created between 1471 and 1480 by Francesco di Lorenzo Rosselli (1445–1513). This is the city that the Medici and Savonarola would have known. (Image via Wikimedia, public domain.)

CHAPTER ONE
FLORENCE BEFORE THE MEDICI

Guelfs and Ghibellines

The Italy of the late Middle Ages and Renaissance was only a geographical expression. The Italian peninsula after the collapse of the Roman Empire in the fifth century was fragmented into a great many independent, often warring states; and with the disintegration of Roman central power, sovereign authority was claimed by both the papacy and by the Germanic emperors. Papal pretensions of universal power resulted from a document known as the Donation of Constantine. The Donation (which first appeared in 778) ostensibly recorded the gift of the Western Empire by Constantine in 315 to Pope Sylvester as thanks for his conversion, baptism, and relief from leprosy, and was accepted as valid from about the eighth century, when it was likely written, until proved to be a forgery during the mid-fifteenth century by the Renaissance humanist Lorenzo Valla. This document justified papal claims of authority on earth, which augmented the already powerful assumption of spiritual authority that resulted from the pope's apostolic succession from St. Peter. The imperial position was that the successors to Roman secular power were the Germanic emperors who claimed sovereignty following the coronation of Charlemagne in St. Peter's Basilica in Rome on Christmas Day, 800. Most of these Holy Roman Emperors (to distinguish them from the ancient rulers of Rome) were German in origin but some, especially during the period of the Hohenstaufen dynasty (1138–1254), resided in Italy and challenged the universal claims of the papacy to both heavenly and earthly power. This conflict between emperor and pope was the foundation of the violent struggles between their adherents: the Guelfs, who accepted the sovereign authority of the pope, and the Ghibellines, who recognized the imperial jurisdiction of the Holy Roman Empire. It would also play a significant role in the development of the Florentine republic, which became one of the leading Guelf cities of north-central Italy.

Florence

By the thirteenth century, Florence was a rapidly growing and increasingly important and rich city in the valley of the river Arno in Tuscany. The wealth of Florence was generated by the production, finishing, and export of woolen cloth of the highest quality and dyed in vibrant colors. The wealth that was produced by this international market and the long-distance trade connections that supported it put Florentine merchants into an ideal position to lend their surplus capital to others, effectively becoming the international bankers of Europe. This opportunity to earn interest on unneeded capital attracted other merchants and even craftsmen to put some of their wealth on deposit with these great mercantile firms, bringing wealth and influence to the entire city, a wealth that did to some degree trickle down to small businessmen and prudent Tuscan families anxious to improve their status and economic position. Furthermore, the expansion of the cloth trade in Florence brought a great many workers from the countryside into the city, increasing both the population and the value of property within the old walls. These factors also had a driving effect on the factional struggles within Florence, which were growing more intense and occasionally violent.

In Tuscany, the division between pope and emperor had a long, complex, and bloody history by the mid-thirteenth century, and the fortunes of both factions fluctuated, depending on the circumstances at a given time and on the policies of individual states, as well as of the papacy and empire. The Ghibellines, supporters of the empire, had initially won a great victory at Montaperti in 1260 where a Florentine Ghibelline army, allied with Siena and Arezzo, slaughtered the Guelf forces of Florence and assumed control of the city. The Guelfs, however, returned to power following the Battle of Benevento in 1266 in which the imperial forces of Manfred of Hohenstaufen were defeated by the Guelfs under Charles of Anjou, king of Sicily, the younger brother of St. Louis IX of France. A papal and French army marched on Florence in 1267 causing the Ghibellines to flee, securing a Guelf administration. Because the Ghibelline faction tended to be more aristocratic, with power in the surrounding feudal countryside, or *contado*, the Guelfs increasingly were associated with new mercantile wealth, favoring social mobility and trade. This resulted in a closer identification between the older mercantile elite and those newly enriched citizens who were anxious to use the power of the commune to further their ambitions.

Although the Ghibellines had been expelled, their houses and property confiscated and their power broken, Florence remained divided by social and economic tensions. Old mercantile Guelf families formed a political organization to ensure a "pure" Guelf Party would dominate the city. This *Parte Guelfa* benefited from a good portion of the wealth taken from the exiled Ghibellines and often shared the almost feudal values of the old nobility whose castles in the countryside were duplicated by huge fortified palaces within the city walls, fortresses surmounted by tall towers that dominated their neighborhoods. Intermarriage and shared values led to the formation of factions, *consorterie* (extended kin networks) and tower societies, organized alliances to support allies and wage urban violence on enemies. The victory of the Guelfs, then, did not bring stability and peace to the city; indeed, the level of urban strife seemed to be increasing, a situation that especially endangered the lesser merchants and shopkeepers who did not have the protection of private towers, bands of armed thugs, and access to power.

What they did enjoy, however, was a growing sense of their economic potential and the recognition that they would need access to government to ensure that their needs would be met. The gold florin had been introduced in 1252 and had rapidly become the standard for international transactions because its value was to be guaranteed by the commune. This pledge had to be kept. Also, there was need for standard weights and measures, well-maintained or expanded city walls, and safe roads. And there needed to be security of property and personal safety in the city for trade and commerce to function. To accomplish these goals, a growing number of Florentine property owners saw some control over the commune as necessary.

By 1280 the city, exploding in new wealth, a growing population, and pressure on space and influence, witnessed sufficient instability that the pope, Nicholas III, recognized the need to secure this important Guelf city and sustain it in the face of growing threats. Charles of Anjou had accepted a ten-year appointment as protector of the city, but by 1277 it was clear that Charles intended to keep some control over Florence in order, he argued, to contain the Ghibelline threat. Pope Nicholas began to see Charles' ambition as similar to the imperial Hohenstaufen's and attempted to broker a peace between the Florentine Guelfs and Ghibellines and to forge a new alliance within the city by supporting the *novi cives*, or those newly enriched citizens who were alienated by the violence and posturing of the old noble families (magnates) and their urban associates (*grandi*), who had intermarried with the magnate clans and adopted their values.

In 1279, the papal legate, Cardinal Latino, the pope's nephew, arrived in Florence and succeeded in brokering a truce between the major Guelf and Ghibelline clans. Many exiled Ghibellines (but not all) were permitted to return and reclaim their property, and a new committee consisting of both Guelfs and Ghibellines, as well as nonaligned citizens, was to be formed. The authority for choosing the fourteen men who would collectively constitute the executive of the government was entrusted to the more substantial guilds in the city. By 1282 this arrangement was challenged by events not in Tuscany but Sicily. The revolt of the Sicilian Vespers required Charles of Anjou to take his army south to protect his Sicilian crown. Florence was no longer under the immediate control of the Angevins, the house of Anjou; seizing the opportunity, the dynamic merchant elite initiated what would amount to a bourgeois coup.

The guildsmen began to choose their own leaders, or priors, to speak for their individual guilds and collective mercantile interests. The most influential guilds were not the craft organizations of small shopkeepers and artisans, but the cartels of international merchants comprising the *arti maggiori* or greater guilds. These were judges and notaries, bankers and money-changers, woolen cloth manufacturers, cloth dealers, silk producers and merchants, apothecaries and physicians, and furriers. All of these guilds were capital intensive and most had international connections, negotiating in markets outside Florentine territory. Not all of those who matriculated in these guilds actually practiced the trade but rather sought influence and connections by associating with the most prominent merchants of Florence.

These leading guildsmen, or priors, were allowed a certain responsibility in the execution of policy, and after 1282 constituted a kind of executive committee of the republic. Because of their economic skill and negotiating talent, these priors assumed responsibility for important aspects of public life, such as overseeing the contracts of the *podestà*, that foreign official hired for one year to command the military and public order agencies of the commune. Military matters remained central to their concerns, as war was omnipresent in the unstable world of late thirteenth-century Tuscany, and the need for civic order was obvious. This was still a period of intense warfare between Guelf and Ghibelline states, witnessed by the Battle of Campaldino in 1289 in which a Guelf army destroyed a Ghibelline force from Arezzo. This victory—in which the poet Dante fought as a young man—ensured Guelf supremacy in the city but left it open to rival factions within the Guelfs themselves.

In that same year, the commune legally abolished all vestiges of feudalism in all Florentine territories. This act, which concluded a process already well under way, had the effect of strengthening the urban authority of Florence by diminishing the power of the old magnate families to recruit private armies from among their peasants and also permitted ambitious young men from the *contado* to migrate to the city to work in the expanding textile industry, ensuring sufficient labor and keeping wages under control through job competition. This legislation and the development of citizen militias organized within all the districts (*quartieri*) of the city afforded the urban mercantile elite a strong position to complete their assumption of power.

The Ordinances of Justice

In January of 1293 their assumption of power was accomplished through a series of laws known as the Ordinances of Justice. Taken together, these cemented the bourgeois coup that had begun the decade before. First, Florence was defined as a guild republic with the seven greater guilds augmented by fourteen lesser guilds (*arti minori*), representing traditional craft guilds. These were butchers, blacksmiths, shoemakers, builders, clothing sellers, vintners, innkeepers, food sellers, tanners, armorers, ironworkers, saddlers and belt makers, carpenters, and bakers. All of these guildsmen represented solid middle- or lower-middle-class Florentines who paid taxes, held property, and usually employed others. Provided they were adults, not in arrears of taxes nor bankrupt, sane, and resident in the city, all of those who had matriculated in these guilds had access to public office.

The fractious and often Ghibelline magnates were controlled by being ineligible to hold communal office, even if a guildsman. Lists of magnates were compiled, amounting to about 150 families. They had to post a bond for good behavior and they could no longer build or maintain their fortified palaces in town, those urban fortresses surmounted by tall towers. These had to be pulled down to a certain height and could never be rebuilt. Crimes committed by magnates were to be prosecuted to the full extent of the law and the responsibility for serious offenses could be applied to other members of a noble clan guilty of violence. A seventh prior was added, the *gonfaloniere della giustizia*, the standard bearer of justice, whose responsibility was to enforce the terms of the Ordinances with the *podestà*; and he was given a thousand men to do so. In short, the magnates—and their urban, mercantile allies of the *grandi* (old rich urban clans who had thrown in their lot with the *magnati*)—were disenfranchised and put on parole as a class, leaving the government of the city to the guildsmen who saw the commune as an instrument for protecting and expanding their wealth and influence, and as a vehicle for their ambitions. It was this constitution that was to guide Florence until the imposition of the Medici duchy in 1530, that is, throughout the period of the Renaissance.

Factional Instability

The humbling of the Ghibellines, the magnates, and *grandi* did not end factional divisions, however. The victorious Guelfs divided into the White and Black factions, characterized by family divisions and depth of obedience to the papacy. In 1301 the Blacks, aided by a French army, took the newly constructed seat of government, the Palazzo della Signoria (today called the Palazzo Vecchio) and installed a Black regime; the Whites and other opponents, including Dante and Petrarch's father, were exiled in January of 1302. This event was to signal the inability of the mercantile elite to sustain a stable polity. Later events were to offer even greater threats to the integrity of the city and the Ordinances.

The fourteenth century was particularly unstable. Florence, under the influence of the Italian Guelfs, accepted the Angevin king Robert of Naples as nominal lord, or *signore*, from 1313 to 1322. Affairs in his own kingdom limited his activity in Florence, but in 1325 the Florentines were severely defeated at Altopascio by the armies of Castruccio Castracani, the lord of Lucca. Fearing the Lucchesi, who were savaging the Florentine *contado*, Florence submitted to the rule of Charles, duke of Calabria, the son of King Robert of Naples. Charles was to enjoy a ten-year lordship over the city, but his time there was not popular, as he saw himself a monarch and cared little for Florentine sensibilities.

In particular he taxed the city heavily, including those patricians who had traditionally rigged the tax rolls in their favor. Charles, however, did not last, as he was more interested in reuniting Sicily to the Neapolitan Angevin crown and serving his father's ambitions in the south. It was with relief that his early death in 1328 was announced, permitting the republican constitution to operate once more.

The failure of Charles of Calabria was not the last experiment with "temporary" lordship in Florence. By the late 1330s, Florence was suffering from a severe economic depression resulting from bad loans to northern European monarchs and the expense of an unsuccessful war again against Lucca. Because the debts were so large and because the Florentine elite craftily shielded themselves from the obvious need for higher taxation, a cabal of wealthy bankers and merchants invited a French nobleman related to the Angevins of Naples, with estates in Greece and Italy, to serve for a time as lord of Florence in order to solve their problems for them. This man on horseback was Walter of Brienne, the duke of Athens. Walter had been in Florence before as a companion and administrator for Charles of Calabria; and it was believed he could be used to protect the interests of the elite while still defeating Lucca and addressing the fiscal imbalance. Walter was elevated in 1342 and came to Florence, again seeing himself as a kind of monarch. Despite a contract that limited his authority and tenure of office, Walter proved very popular among the disenfranchised poor of Florence, the laborers in the woolen industry, known collectively as Ciompi. These Ciompi proclaimed Walter ruler for life and it appeared that Florence would follow so many of the other Italian communes into a monarchical or tyrannical regime.

Walter, however, proved to be overly tyrannical, imposing harsh taxes, especially on the rich, and ruling without reference to the laws of Florence. His imposition of the *estimo* (a wealth tax) on all citizens with property, and his unwillingness to repay the forced loans required of the elite, alienated his regime from the very group that had imported him into the city initially. His popularity with the Ciompi was also a disadvantage because it reinforced his image as a foreigner intent on making Florence a monarchy at the expense of the traditional political classes. In 1343 a conspiracy of important citizens drove him forever from the city.

It is ironic that Walter had been summoned by a cabal of powerful merchant families, such as the international banking clan of the Peruzzi, to deal with a financial crisis that was eroding their wealth and hence their influence. Walter did nothing to stop the collapse of the

Florentine—and soon the European—banking system occasioned by the default of King Edward III of England on the huge debts the crown owed to Florentine bankers. The great banking houses of the Bardi and Peruzzi were owed 900,000 and 600,000 florins, respectively; and with Edward's default their companies and the other large bank of the Acciaiuoli family essentially collapsed between 1343 and 1346, bringing down with them the thousands of investors, large and small, who had placed their wealth on deposit in hopes of strong returns. Edward, moreover, compounded the crisis by confiscating the property of the Italians and exiling them from his kingdom.

A New Civic Ethos

The economic situation in Florence by 1343 was desperate as a consequence, but in this instance the Florentine elite confronted the situation themselves rather than hope that a foreign lord would solve the crisis and go away. What emerged was one of the most sophisticated forms of fiscal policy yet devised. The vast and widely distributed debt of the commune of Florence was amalgamated into a single fund, or Monte. This debt was then serviced by granting holders of the debt—or those who later bought into it—shares which initially promised a return of 5 percent. The effect was revitalizing. Access to capital by the commune rose almost 300 percent in just forty years, restoring the finances of the city. The coming of the Black Death in 1348 challenged this recovery in many ways by reducing demand for Florentine woolens and financial services, by driving up wages for those who survived, and by dislocating production through the loss of skilled workers. But economics is the dismal science, so there was in fact a silver lining in this catastrophe. It is estimated that half of the population of Florence died in the years 1348–1350, a true demographic nightmare. But those who survived were much wealthier, regardless of their position. Ciompi and other workers could command higher wages, especially if skilled, and the patrician elite of the city who survived the plague saw the wealth of their dead relatives funneled down to the survivors through the so-called "inheritance effect." Businesses shaken by the bank failures and the loss of markets were now recapitalized, able to employ workers, pay taxes, and move into other, more lucrative spheres. The tragedy of the Black Death actually helped Florence recover over time.

Politically, the peril to republican freedom and guild rule represented by the tyranny of Walter of Brienne and the collapse of some of the powerful families that had invited him to Florence galvanized the political classes to experiment with a broader-based regime, rather than look for ways to manage the city through oligarchy or external authority. The guildsmen of the lesser guilds, *arti minori*, were brought more actively into the *signoria*, holding official positions proportionate to their greater numbers. A new sense of balance and cooperation began to operate, and the city, lubricated by Monte shares, functioned much more effectively. Indeed, the establishment of the Monte had a profound effect because the policies of the commune influenced the wealth of those holding shares in the funded debt, changing their attitude toward policy and government: a greater proportion of the population was now directly affected by communal policy. These citizens took a more active interest in the commune as a whole and not just in their own guild, neighborhood, or extended clan. A new concept of the state was emerging.

New Urban Space

During the years between the promulgation of the Ordinances of Justice and the mid-fourteenth century the city was also growing and changing physically, becoming ever more beautiful and proud. The guild republic required a place to meet and centralize the offices of state; hence, Arnolfo di Cambio, a genius from Val di Col d'Elsa, was called upon to build the Palazzo della Signoria (now Palazzo Vecchio), which opened at the beginning of the century and is still the city hall of Florence. A new cathedral was also designed by Arnolfo, Santa Maria del Fiore, to replace the small, early Christian basilica of Santa Reparata. The Franciscan preaching church of Santa Croce arose as did the Dominican church of Santa Maria Novella, designed in this case by a Dominican monk. Giotto was brought to the city to paint the Bardi and Peruzzi chapels in Santa Croce in the 1320s, and Giotto was commissioned to design the bell tower of the new cathedral. Andrea Pisano was commissioned in 1330 to create bronze doors for the Romanesque baptistery of the cathedral, completing them in 1336; after Giotto's death, he was given the responsibility for the *campanile*. A new set of walls was in place by 1333 that allowed for a protected population of as many as 100,000, even if those walls were not altogether filled until Florence briefly became the capital of a united Italy in 1865. This concrete change in the urban design and public monuments of the city increased the sense of civic pride felt by most citizens, adding to their self-confidence and perception that change was happening and for the better.

Between 1293 and 1350 the urban character of the city had changed dramatically. What had been at the end of the thirteenth century a city of spiky, noble towers, symbolizing public power in private hands, Florence had become by the mid-fourteenth century a grand metropolis identified by the public towers of the community, the collective of citizens active in the republic. Some towers represented the city as a polis: the towers on the Palazzo della Signoria and on the Bargello (the palace of the *podestà*, erected in 1250). Others represented the Christian community, so closely linked with the idea of citizenship: the bell tower of Giotto on the cathedral, the spires of the Badia di Firenze (the Florentine abbey near the Piazza della Signoria), and on other churches. The message was clear: public power now resided in collective, public hands, operating through the guild republic, a republic able to withstand the challenges of *signori*, plague, financial collapse, and political factionalism.

This broadly based and largely successful experiment with guild republicanism was challenged once more, again as a consequence of war and economic upheaval. In 1375 Florence was at war with the papacy, then resident in Avignon. The effect of this conflict—the War of the Eight Saints—was to disrupt Florence's trade and banking operations. Florence had traditionally benefited from its position as the leading Guelf city in central Italy by serving as a papal banker, transferring money and sourcing loans. This account was obviously lost. Also, the pope used spiritual weapons very effectively: excommunicating Florentines, ordering Catholics not to trade with them, confiscating their property, and treating them as enemies of God and the Church. The effect on the woolen industry was disastrous, as many northern European markets evaporated, resulting in widespread unemployment among the approximately 10,000 wool workers in the city. These men—and some women—were paid through piecework in a complex putting-out system that often resulted in workers becoming indebted to their employers. Furthermore, they were often brutally treated by their overseers. By 1378 the atmosphere was one of anger and despair.

The Ciompi Revolt and the Age of Oligarchy

Figure 2. The Palazzo della Signoria was commissioned in 1299 as the site of the communal government following the Ordinances of Justice (1293). The architect was Arnolfo di Cambio, who was also responsible for the new cathedral (Santa Maria del Fiore). It is now called the Palazzo Vecchio (Old Palace) because the first Medici hereditary grand duke of Tuscany (Cosimo I) moved his court to the Palazzo Pitti in the 1550s. (Image via Wikimedia, CC BY-SA 3.0 license.)

An unscrupulous patrician, Salvestro de' Medici, afraid of losing political power to his enemies, worked to stir up this resentment, eventually convincing them to attack the palaces of his factional opponents. Once this tumult began, however, others in the city joined the rioting, especially those semi-skilled workers denied guild membership and hence access to political office. From this mob arose a remarkable, natural leader: Michele di Lando, an overseer in the woolen industry. With some renegade patricians and Michele's leadership ability, a new government committee was called to reform the communal government. Three new guilds were added, including one for the poor, often illiterate Ciompi, the Guild of Lesser Citizens (*Arte del popolo minuto*). The new guilds of those previously disenfranchised numbered about 12,000 men, outnumbering by a factor of three the total guild membership of the original twenty-one guilds, whose numbers tended to hover just over about 4,000 citizens. Michele di Lando became the standard bearer of justice (*gonfaloniere della giustizia*).

This situation angered and alarmed the traditional political elite, as they had no intention of seeing Ciompi chosen as priors and living with them in the Palazzo della Signoria for the required two months of office.

Equally, the lesser guildsmen, whose wealth was concentrated in their shops and stock, saw the dangers of riot, which could lead to arson and looting. Furthermore, they feared a spike in wages in hard times, if the poor had an opportunity to influence communal policy and guild legislation. So, the lesser guildsmen made common cause with the greater guildsmen of the *arti maggiori* and agreed to let them lead the commune once more if their property and economic well-being could be protected. The elite used promises and bribes to compromise Michele di Lando, so by 1381 most of the Ciompi Revolt's gains had been abrogated, including the new guilds. An even harsher regime was imposed on the workers, with the importation of foreign, usually Flemish, overseers, who did not even speak Italian. What suffered most, however, was the sense of integrity and shared values that had characterized the commune between 1343 and 1378.

After the Ciompi Revolt, the far more numerous lesser guildsmen yielded to the patricians in return for stability and security; and the patricians began to forge an oligarchic regime. This oligarchy did not overturn the measures of the Ordinances of Justice, but merely ignored or undermined them. Magnate and *grandi* families were permitted into guild and communal office through the fiction of just changing their names; the *divieto*, that law that excluded several members of a family from holding high office simultaneously, was not enforced; and the leading wealthy patricians were invited to give "advice" through formal consultations known as *Consulte e Pratiche*; however, the advice was very often direction, despite the fact that those invited did not hold any elected office.

Moreover, this oligarchic regime, led by the Albizzi family and hence known as the Albizzi Oligarchy, did what all oligarchies eventually do: restrict membership to make the ruling elite a very small club consisting of men and families who used the commune for their own benefit, even to the detriment of good policy. Eventually, again as with all oligarchies, opposition from below and from outside the closed elite began to coalesce around powerful individuals and groups. Weary of a debilitating and unsuccessful—and witheringly expensive—war against Lucca, angry at their continued exclusion from office, and the policies of the commune that favored the businesses of the great international merchants at the expense of the local economy, lesser guildsmen and some patricians began to organize an opposition. The natural leader of this anti-oligarchic faction was an unusual choice: Cosimo de'Medici, Il Vecchio (the Elder), perhaps the richest man in Europe and one of considerable experience, a man whose sympathy was with the institutions of the republic and so had little desire to be drawn into the oligarchy. Cosimo's rise and the fear it engendered among the oligarchs would indeed lead to a new regime in 1434, occasioned by a clumsy attempt to neutralize Cosimo through false testimony, an unfair trial for treason, and exile. This assault on the leader of the popular faction would spark the very revolt the oligarchs feared most, and in 1434 Cosimo would return to his city and begin the long period of the Medici hegemony.

CHAPTER TWO
THE MEDICI HEGEMONY (1434–1494)

The Medici and Its Bank

The Medici were not among the oldest, richest, or most respected families in Florence during the first century of the republic. Originally from the poor agricultural region of the Mugello, the family only seems to have migrated to Florence by the late twelfth century. No Medici appears in any document before the early thirteenth century, and the records of their wealth reveal a comfortable fortune, but hardly spectacular; and some of the family's many branches were assessed at very low levels of taxation. Nor were the Medici prominent in the most prestigious appointments or elected positions in the commune. Until the late fourteenth century, then, the Medici could not compete with the great established political clans, like the Alberti, Strozzi, or Bardi, even though it was clear the family was gaining in wealth in influence.

All of this changed with the success of Giovanni di Bicci de'Medici. His training began as a factor in his uncle's bank in Rome, which gave him both experience and contacts with the papal court. He started his own company, with branches in Florence, Venice, Naples, and Rome, but it was the Roman connection that resulted in his remarkable ascendance to great wealth. The years from 1378 until 1417 saw the division of the church as a consequence of the Great Western Schism. From 1378 until 1409 there were two popes, one in Avignon and one in Rome; after a failed attempt to end the schism in 1409–10, there were three popes, as cardinals from both colleges had elected one of their number on the understanding that the other two pontiffs would resign or be deposed. That did not happen and the ultimate absurdity for Christendom emerged with a fragmented church and papacy. Although this situation was a spiritual trauma for devout Christians, it was seen as an opportunity for the Medici bank.

A successor to the pope elected in Pisa in 1410 was Baldassare Cossa, a man with a disreputable past but much political skill and ambition,

Figure 3. Cosimo de'Medici, Il Vecchio (the elder, to distinguish him from Cosimo I, grand duke of Tuscany) by Jacopo Pontormo (1494–1556). It was painted almost sixty years after Cosimo's death but alludes to the symbols and styles of the 1460s. Cosimo is shown in profile, a reference to ancient Roman coins and medals, and dressed in his usual sober red costume. The plant beside him is one with a reputation for hardiness, which, despite its treatment, will root again and bloom. (Image via Wikimedia, public domain.)

who took the title John XXIII. (He was subsequently declared an anti-pope; consequently, his papal name could be reused in 1958 by St. John XXIII.) His banker was Giovanni di Bicci de'Medici. Until John's deposition in 1415, the Medici bank was responsible for almost all elements of the financial dealings of those parts of the Church under John's control, claiming a substantial commission but also gaining important connections both in Rome and throughout Europe. Moreover, the return of a united papacy under Martin V to Rome in 1420 provided even more opportunities to exploit the Medici bank's experience in papal finances. Thus, by the 1420s the Medici bank was one of the largest and best connected on the continent and Giovanni one of the richest men. At the time of his death in 1429 he was one of the wealthiest citizens in the city of Florence.

Giovanni de'Bicci also prepared for the rise of his family in Florence. Although he had often refused election to public office, both because it could interfere with his business and because he feared becoming embroiled in the notoriously fractious politics of the republic, he did serve in the highest office of *gonfaloniere della giustizia* in 1424; his international connections had resulted in his being sent on several important embassies. Although his own interest in politics was limited, he recognized how important public office would be for the future of his family. The Florentine obsession with honor and reputation, illustrated through holding high elective positions in the commune, being invited to advise the Signoria, and contracting marriage alliances with old, powerful families, meant that his son, Cosimo, needed to be prepared to raise the reputation of the Medici in the city. It was also a prudent way to protect the family's wealth and property, as Giovanni had begun to invest in the traditional woolen industry as well as acquiring agricultural estates in the *contado*. It was on this platform of wealth and reputation that his son, Cosimo, would build and eventually become the founder of the Medici family's hegemony in the city of Florence.

Cosimo de'Medici, Il Vecchio

Giovanni di Bicci prepared his son carefully for the role he would be expected to play in Florentine government and society. His education was managed in such a way that Cosimo would come to represent the new, dynamic environment of humanistic studies then becoming established as the elite educational and cultural program for the mercantile patriciate in Florence. Although he did not know Greek, Cosimo developed an interest in Platonic philosophy and counted the philosopher Marsilio Ficino and the Greek scholar Manuel Chrysoloras among his friends. The humanist scholar Poggio Bracciolini had first encountered Cosimo at the Council of Constance in 1414 and the two became friends, with Cosimo even liquidating the debts of that one-time papal secretary to John XXIII and assisting with his search for neglected ancient texts. Cosimo himself was an obsessive collector of manuscripts, endowing several libraries, and commissioning hundreds of excellent editions from Vespasiano di Bisticci, the Florentine stationer who later became his biographer. And he helped Niccolo Niccoli, the celebrated humanist bibliophile, to build the collection that would later form the nucleus of the Laurentian Library (because it was located in the cloister of the Medici church of San Lorenzo).

But Cosimo was in essence a banker, and his wealth and growing prestige compelled him to engage in the fractious politics of his city. The death of his father, Giovanni di Bicci, in 1429 thrust him into the center of Florentine political activity. He was now the most respected and wealthiest member of an extended kin and patronage network that was recognized as an alternative faction by those who opposed the Albizzi Oligarchy. The oligarchy had declined in influence after the death of

Maso degli Albizzi (1417), whose political skill and authority were not inherited by his son Rinaldo. Moreover, the war with Lucca was not only going badly but was devouring large amounts of money—money that had to be raised through the taxation of wealthy citizens. To the exposed Albizzi faction, Cosimo was a serious threat.

The danger posed by Cosimo arose not only from his wealth and the respect he generated in the city, but also from the very nature of the Florentine republican constitution. Sortition and election on a frequent basis ensured a high rotation of officials in the highest offices of the Signoria. The eight priors and *gonfaloniere della giustizia*, for example, held their executive committee positions for only two months and then were ineligible for reelection for another three years. Consequently, it was inevitable that a majority of Medici supporters would eventually be elected, giving Cosimo an opportunity to neutralize the oligarchs, but the election of a pro-Albizzi Signoria provided the motivation to remove Cosimo and other members of his family from Florence. So, in September of 1433 the oligarchs decided to preempt the threat from the Medici. Cosimo was summoned to the Signoria and imprisoned there for a month before a sentence of ten years' exile was pronounced, made more stringent through the levy of a large surety and the exile of his close relatives. The Albizzi had pressed hard for Cosimo's execution, but the Medici had too many influential supporters in the city and elsewhere in Italy for this to be possible. The pope, the republic of Venice, and the rulers of several Italian principalities made it clear that they would not look indifferently on the death of Cosimo. Consequently, the sentence was exile first to Padua and then to Venice.

Cosimo had to a degree anticipated some kind of action against him. He took the precaution of transferring much of his bank's assets to other branches and his personal fortune into the name of his supporters and the accounts of powerful religious institutions. He knew he would need his wealth and realized that the oligarchs would attempt to deprive him of his fortune. He also sustained a complex network of friends and supporters within and outside Florence. These could provide information and agitate for his return, once the process of elections revealed a more sympathetic Signoria and the political, fiscal, and military failures of the oligarchy alienated ever more citizens.

Cosimo's time came almost exactly a year after he was first summoned to the Palazzo della Signoria. In August of 1434 a Signoria with a

Medici plurality was chosen, despite the illegal and increasingly desperate attempts on the part of the Albizzi faction to subvert the process. The new government immediately called for a *Parlamento*, the body in which Florentine political sovereignty resides, consisting of the adult male heads of all households. The ringing of the great bell, known as *La Vacca* (the cow), in the tower of the palace required citizens to assemble in the Piazza della Signoria. Fearing violence or an attempted coup, the Medici supporters had brought in armed men to keep order, but there was no need. The pope, Eugene IV Condulmer, was in the city and called for calm and due process, and the oligarchs did not enjoy enough support to take the city by force. Thus, the *Parlamento* obediently approved a list of members for a special commission (*Balìa*) to address the situation in the city. Word was spread that only the leaders of the oligarchy would suffer serious punishment, as was appropriate, but the majority of supporters of the Albizzi Oligarchy had little to fear. The result was that Cosimo was recalled and returned to Florence in October of 1434, welcomed by the majority of citizens of all classes.

The Hegemony of Cosimo il Vecchio (1434–1464)

Cosimo's return offered him and his faction a number of immediate opportunities. The Albizzi oligarchs had been defeated and subsequently exiled, and the Medici enjoyed wide support in the city among all political classes. Moreover, that extraordinary time necessitated some extraordinary measures. The lists of citizens eligible for office and the names collected for inclusion in the bags for selection were destroyed to begin the new regime with a clean slate and to cleanse the electoral system of any residual elements of Albizzi supporters. A commission agreed to temporarily restrict the number of names placed in the electoral bags, and Medici partisans were chosen as *accoppiatori*, the officials who scrutinized citizens' suitability for office and loaded names in the bags. These measures were intended as temporary, needed to bring some stability to the communal government after the events of 1433–1434, but it must also be interpreted as a cunning method of electoral manipulation to ensure the predominance of the Medici faction. It was necessary, as Cosimo recognized, that the means of control be subtle because Florence remained altogether republican in its political culture, an ideology which humanist chancellors, such as Leonardo Bruni (chancellor 1427–1444) had enshrined as the essence of the republic's character. His *History of Florence* and *Panegyric of Florence* (*Laudatio Urbis Florentinae*) defined the collective character of the city's essence as its thirst for liberty, republican freedom, and the struggle against oppression within the city and in its foreign policy. And, it must be said, Cosimo himself understood and indeed apparently harbored some sympathy for these ideals of republicanism and freedom. Once back in 1434 he was in a position to restructure the communal administration in fundamental ways, but he chose instead to manipulate the structures already in place. By controlling the *accoppiatori*, continuing to limit access to office to smaller groups of citizens, and establishing mechanisms to influence the large councils of the republic, Cosimo was able to exert his will but in a relatively discreet manner, and thus not offend the sensibilities of the political classes who could oppose his policies. Similarly, he knew that he could not alienate the great mass of disenfranchised citizens: the memory of the revolt was still current, and Cosimo was devoted to building a stable regime that would last and be insulated from the usual factional struggles that had compromised the city's wealth and unity.

Furthermore, Cosimo achieved this balance during a particularly dangerous period in Italian affairs. The last Visconti duke had made war on an alliance consisting of Venice, the states of the Church, and Florence, and a number of influential Florentines, exiled in 1434 as supporters of the Albizzi, had joined the Milanese. At Anghiari in 1440 the Milanese were defeated, a victory that would lead to Leonardo da Vinci's commission for a commemorative fresco in the Palazzo Vecchio in 1503. The war was a closely fought engagement, and the alliance's victory was seen as another example of Florence having been victorious against great odds because of its belief in freedom and liberty. This was not a time to seriously dismantle the republican constitution.

That said, however, the war was expensive and there was the desperate need for higher taxation for all classes of citizens. Thus, the manipulation of the electoral lists continued, as did the restrictions on eligible citizens for office. Cosimo could not risk a strong opposition at such a dangerous moment; he might have appreciated the republican principles of the political classes and the traditional hostility toward Milan, but he was a pragmatist and understood extremely well the necessity of managing the situation in the city.

Beginning in 1423, Florence, as an ally of Venice against Milan, had been drawn into a series of conflicts that resulted from the clash of Milanese and Venetian ambitions, mostly in Lombardy. These wars at one time or another not only involved Florence, Milan, and Venice, but also the papacy, Naples, and many of the small principalities in north-central Italy. The campaigns were conducted by *condottieri*, mercenary captains who fought for whatever side engaged them or paid the most, and they often changed sides. Of the successful captains in these wars, Francesco Sforza stands out as one who served Florence, Milan, Venice, and the pope, reflecting the traditional flexibility of allegiance characteristic of mercenaries.

The issue of Milan illustrated the continued instability of the Italian peninsula. The main line of the Visconti had come to an end in 1447 with the death of Duke Filippo Maria. He left only a natural daughter, Bianca, who was married to Francesco Sforza. There was a brief and unsuccessful attempt to establish a republican regime (the Ambrosian Republic), but Sforza laid siege and captured Milan in 1450, claiming the title of duke, much to the unhappiness of the Milanese republicans and the Holy Roman Emperor who, in theory, had the right to name the ruler, as Milan was technically an imperial fief. Sforza had been supported by Cosimo de'Medici: not only had they formed an understanding based on mutual ambition during Sforza's service to Florence but they also realized that a weak Milan would further encourage Venetian incursions into Lombardy, which could threaten both Milan and Florence.

Sforza's success in establishing his rule in Milan consequently resulted in a major and profound shift in Florentine policy, a shift that reflected the relationship between Cosimo and Francesco: Florence formed an alliance with Milan against Venice. From at least the wars of Giangaleazzo Visconti in the late fourteenth century, Milan was identified as the greatest danger to republican freedom and Florentine security. The Viper of Milan (the Visconti arms were a serpent devouring a baby) represented, in the humanist invective and diplomatic correspondence of chancellors like Salutati and Bruni, the antithesis of Florentine republicanism and liberty. Now, Milan was attached to Florence in alliance against another republic, Venice. There was much hostility to this dramatic pivot in foreign policy among the Florentine political elite, providing they thought evidence that the Medici, by associating with tyrants, might have similar ambitions themselves, particularly as Francesco Sforza's powerful army would now be at Cosimo's disposal.

This reconfiguration of the traditional alliance system in Italy also forced the Venetians and their Neapolitan allies to negotiate rather than fight. It was now evident that no state had sufficient strength to establish hegemony in the peninsula, so a structure that would create a balance of power was more realistic. The consequence of this remarkable diplomatic effort was the Peace of Lodi of 1454. All of the five major Italian states (Venice, Milan, Florence, the States of the Church, and Naples) recognized spheres of influence in which they might operate freely, but if one major state attacked another or interfered too egregiously in the sphere of another, then the remaining signatories would restore the balance of power. And, Francesco Sforza and his successors were recognized as the legitimate rulers of the duchy of Milan. This treaty was enlarged the following year with the creation of the Italian League (1455), which promised joint military action against any invasion from outside Italy. A mature and thoughtful policy of peace and collective security began to bring a measure of stability and cooperation to the peninsula, granting Cosimo and Francesco Sforza time to put down deep roots for their regimes.

The Peace of Lodi had another effect in Florence: there was now increased agitation to end the Medici's policy of manipulating the republic's political life by restricting the number of men eligible for office. The arguments for the need of security and stability evaporated, as did the belief that only a managed Signoria could provide the necessary high tax levies that were required to hire armies to protect the republic. Cosimo and his faction realized this and conceded that there needed to be a more open process of choosing elected officials. Anger at the continued manipulation of the *borse* (bags containing the names of eligible guildsmen) had begun to stir unrest to the point of engendering a plot against the Medici in 1457. Although it was discovered and its leaders executed or exiled, Cosimo's reluctant agreement to tolerate an expanded political class had been challenged, a situation exacerbated by the lack of consensus among his faction and other leading citizens as to how open the republic should be to all eligible citizens.

The conspiracy against him and the recognition that the dangers of divisive factional politics might make the city once more unstable (and hence vulnerable), together with the need to sustain higher taxation to recover from the period before 1454, at last drove Cosimo in 1458 to agree to a change in the constitution, although not one that would be automatically interpreted as the creation of a tyranny or even a much more managed political system. Through a *Balìa*, the citizens of Florence accepted the creation of a new council, the *Consiglio dei Cento*, or Council of One Hundred, elected from new lists of citizens and able to assume responsibility for particular, important administrative and policy functions; nevertheless, this body had to have its policies accepted by the two older councils (that of the People and of the Commune). Furthermore, the *accoppiatori* were again to draw up restricted lists of eligible citizens, returning Florence to the *governo stretto* (narrow administration) that had characterized Medici rule since 1434. It was this modified and carefully managed constitution that would characterize the Florentine commune until Cosimo's death in 1464.

Although there was naturally still opposition to the Medici and to Cosimo himself, it did not seriously endanger the regime. Cosimo labored not to appear overtly ambitious, nor did he unnecessarily affront the exquisite egos and family pride of the great families through shows of arbitrary action or vainglory, even if in his last decade he increasingly summoned officials to his palace rather than meet them in the halls of the Palazzo della Signoria. He held office only when elected, and his return to the highest offices in the republic was just what a rich and respected citizen could expect, nothing more. He dressed soberly and continued to use his wealth to benefit and embellish the city, and he seemed to most Florentines to have brought a new age of stability and order to a notoriously fractious and apparently ungovernable city. It was from a sincere feeling of loss and respect that Cosimo was granted the title of *Pater Patriae* on his death—the elegant classical epithet once given to Cicero, and which still today marks his tomb by Verrocchio near the altar in the family church of San Lorenzo.

Cosimo's success was the result of his personality and patronage, as well as his political machinations. His enormous wealth permitted him to build a large and effective clientage. Through low—or no—interest loans, which were often forgiven, or through helping others find appropriate positions, marriage partners, or business associates, Cosimo constructed a wide network of citizens of every political class who owed him some measure of gratitude. He helped with political and financial problems, and it was broadly believed that he was a good person to know and was

Figure 4. Brunelleschi, The Old Sacristy in the Church of San Lorenzo. The rebuilding of San Lorenzo began under Giovanni di Bicci in 1419 and was continued by his son Cosimo. Brunelleschi constructed the sacristy between 1421 and 1440, with decorative elements by Donatello. It holds the tombs of Giovanni di Bicci de'Medici and Piccarda Bueri, by Buggiano, and the porphyry and bronze sarcophagus of Giovanni and Piero de'Medici by Verrocchio. (Image via Wikimedia, CC-BY 3.0 license.)

worthy of respect. To be his enemy made the marriage of children more difficult and business partnerships more challenging. Those "new men" (*novi cives*), anxious to be admitted into a guild so that they may hold public office and enter the restricted world of Florentine society, knew that his recommendation helped greatly in their matriculation (especially in an *arte minore*), and foreign princes and governments equally recognized the value of having him as a friend, if they wanted to influence public policy. He was generous with his friends—even to the extent of tolerating serious crimes—but could be vindictive to his most vocal enemies, although he would soften if they showed remorse and came around to his position. He was affable to most men and devoted to his family. He had dignity and great intelligence, as well as an obvious and sincere love of his native city. In some ways he was not an easy man to dislike, even if some, like his friend and stationer, Vespasiano da Bisticci, could legitimately remark that he was the commune's puppeteer.

Cosimo as a Patron of Culture

One of the policies that Cosimo practiced most effectively was the patronage of learning, art, and architecture. Cosimo was himself not a very learned man, as his early activity had been directed toward his family business of banking. That said, he did start acquiring books early and enjoyed the company of humanist scholars. His strongest intellectual interest, however, was classical philosophy and patristic authors. Like others of his generation, he saw the recovery of the ancient world as seamlessly interwoven with the texts of the early church, and his subsequent interest in Platonism was inspired as much by St. Augustine as by the academy. Curiously, though, he showed little affinity for *belles lettres*, rhetoric, or ancient history. His mind was speculative, which in a banker was unusual—and even more so in the boss of the Medici faction's political machine. It was this interest that resulted in his support of a group of scholars who were inspired by lectures and discussions held by the Byzantine George Gemistus Plethon in 1438, an intellectual movement strongly reinforced by the presence of large numbers of Greek scholars from Constantinople in Florence. This council called to heal the schism between the western Latin and Eastern Orthodox churches to encourage European intervention against the Ottomans then threatening the Byzantine capital. Cosimo's curiosity about Platonism was further stimulated by his acquaintance with the Byzantine emperor, John VIII Palaeologus, and some of his court, lodged in the Peruzzi palaces in Florence during the council.

By 1459 Cosimo had discovered the remarkable abilities of the young Marsilio Ficino, the son of his physician, who was then studying Greek with the learned Byzantine John Agyropoulos in Florence. In 1462 Cosimo provided the young scholar with use of a villa at Careggi and Greek manuscripts so that he might begin the translation of the entire corpus of Plato's work into Latin, a task completed by 1469, after Cosimo's death. Around Ficino, and to a degree Cosimo, there arose a coterie of learned men equally fascinated with the study of Plato and Platonism, as well as some of the mystical texts associated at that time with this tradition, works such as the Hermetic Books, then attributed to the murky figure of Hermes Trismegistus (Hermes the Thrice Blest). The academy really reached its maturity under Cosimo's grandson Lorenzo the Magnificent when it drew into its discussions men such as Lorenzo himself,

Count Giovanni Pico della Mirandola, Angelo Poliziano, Sandro Botticelli, and even perhaps the young Michelangelo.

In terms of architecture, painting, and sculpture, Cosimo was at once a typical wealthy member of his class with obligations to the public buildings and spaces of the city through guild, confraternity, and committee service, and a discerning patron of public and private art and architecture. He was, for example, on the commission that chose the architect for the lantern of the completed dome of Florence's cathedral (1436). Wisely, the commission chose the dome's creator, Filippo Brunelleschi, although he died before it was finished: this was the work of Michelozzo, the builder of Cosimo's new great palace on the Via Larga (now Via Cavour). The plan for the palace emerged in the decade after the return of Cosimo from exile, and initially Brunelleschi was to be the architect. However, it is said that Cosimo objected to the grandeur of Brunelleschi's design, observing that it was inappropriate for a simple citizen. Although there is a ring of truth in this, inasmuch as Cosimo would not want to affront the competitive and jealous nature of his fellow patricians, it is likely more the case that Cosimo and Brunelleschi did not get along. Brunelleschi was notoriously difficult and he seldom paid court to his patrons, whereas Cosimo wanted a plan that clearly reflected his wishes and needs. Consequently, when the palace was begun in 1444, it was Michelozzo, a pupil of Lorenzo Ghiberti,

Figure 5. Palazzo Medici (now Medici-Ricardi) was commissioned by Cosimo de'Medici from Michelozzo, and was built between 1444 and 1484. Despite its massive size, the palace blends into the streetscape through its use of varied styles in the three stories of the elevation, even if the rusticated stonework on the ground floor seems more reminiscent of earlier times. (Image via Wikimedia, public domain.)

who was the genius behind it. Cosimo was evidently impressed because Michelozzo became his favorite builder: he was given the commissions for the Badia di Fiesole and the reconstruction of the monastery of San Marco.

To decorate the chapel of his new palace, Cosimo engaged Benozzo Gozzoli to fresco the walls with a narrative of the Journey of the Magi. The work is in the International Gothic style and contains stylized portraits of the Medici family down to Cosimo's grandchildren, the Florentine *contado*, and Medici villas. The theme is appropriate because the Medici family were active in the Confraternity of the Magi, so the inclusion of the family would seem an elegant reference. Completed in 1461, this fresco cycle emerges as one of the iconic tributes to Cosimo's patronage.

Similarly, in 1438 he engaged the Dominican monk-artist Fra Angelico to decorate the rebuilt cells and refectory of the monastery San Marco, near the new Medici palace. In addition to frescoing the large cell kept for Cosimo for his personal devotions, he painted the altarpiece of the monastery, *Saints Cosmas and Damian Healing Palladia* (1438–1440). This, too, is a reference to Cosimo, as he took his namesake physician Saint Cosmas as a personal protector. This commission reveals Cosimo's range of patronage. In his chapel, for example, he accepted the advice of his son Piero and chose Benozzo Gozzoli as his painter in 1449; he also employed Gentile da Fabriano, like Benozzo a master of the International Gothic style—a style that looked back and north. However, in San Marco he employed the somewhat avant-garde painter Fra Angelico, whose use of linear perspective and composition was inspired by Masaccio. And, probably again in conjunction with Piero, he may have commissioned the three panels of *The Battle of San Romano* from the eccentric genius Paolo Uccello, an artist of such originality and control of perspective that he is almost in a category of his own. Thus, Cosimo as a patron cannot altogether be identified as either conservative or cutting edge in painting or architecture: he was broad in his taste and he enjoyed a discerning eye for genius.

In sculpture, however, he was very committed to the radical new style and technical skill of masters such as Donatello, who became a friend. Indeed, it is hard to overestimate the importance of Donatello in the development of Florentine Renaissance sculpture. He cast the bronze *David* (c. 1440s) for the courtyard of Cosimo's new palace, creating the first free-standing male nude figure since antiquity and defining a recurring symbol of the Florentine Republic. His *Judith and Holofernes*

Figure 6. The Journey of the Magi, Benozzo Gozzoli (c. 1421–1497) was commissioned to fresco the chapel in the Medici palace between 1459 and 1461 by Cosimo de'Medici and his son Piero. The International Gothic style permits a vast number of crowded figures, including stylized Medici portraits, the emperor of Byzantium, and a self-portrait of Benozzo himself, with his name on his hat. The theme is appropriate because of the Medici patronage of the Confraternity of the Magi. (Image via Wikimedia, public domain.)

(c. 1460) was to be mounted on a fountain in the garden of the palace. Like David, Judith is a symbol of freedom and courage, representing the Medici as protectors of the liberty of Florence. Similarly, Donatello was commissioned to cast the bronze pulpits in the Medici church of San Lorenzo, as well as the painted terracotta images—including another Cosmas and Damian—and the bronze doors of the Old Sacristy, the burial place of Cosimo's family.

Cosimo's patronage of art, architecture, and scholarship must be seen as part of his overall policy for Medici control in Florence. He had the wealth to make his city beautiful and famous for its culture. This constituted in the Italian Renaissance the equivalence of war by other means, as competition for artists and celebrated creations was intense and often personal. The reputation of a city could be established through the brilliance of a royal court, military victories, or the raising of public monuments, reminiscent of the Rome of Augustus, whose famous quote that he had found a city of brick but left a city of marble was often rehearsed. Furthermore, as a subtle manipulator of the republic, Cosimo could establish his own legitimacy, generosity, cultivation, and influence within the city through patronage. The Medici were to be seen as the guarantors of the city's liberty and fame. In this way Cosimo's patronage constitutes a form of family propaganda and another instrument of political manipulation, but the effects are truly magnificent. Florence itself developed into a work of art because of his commissions, and citizens of all classes could rejoice in the ornamentation of the city, its power to attract geniuses in all fields, and its growing reputation, all of which were in part delivered by Medici money and Medici patronage.

Piero di Cosimo, "Il Gottoso" (the Gouty, 1464–1469)

It is an indication of the respect with which the Florentines held Cosimo, and hence the Medici, that his son Piero was widely expected to assume his father's influence in the city. Piero, however, was not his father. He was forty-eight in 1464, the year Cosimo died, and had not been very prominent in the city's affairs. He did, of course, hold office when elected and the Signoria sought his voice when appropriate. His splendid humanist education should have admitted him to the elite culture of his father's coterie, but he appeared to have little interest in Platonism or the philosophical speculation for which Cosimo was known. He had a very keen eye for art and indeed was probably the true agency behind the Benozzo Gozzoli and Paolo Uccello commissions; in sculpture he patronized Verrocchio who cast his *David* for Piero, a great work, although hardly as startlingly innovative as that of Donatello. Mostly his interests were in those ancient *objets de vertu*: cameos, small bronzes, gems, and other cabinet objects, an obsession he would pass on to his son, Lorenzo.

Piero's great disadvantage, however, was his health. Long before his father's death, the gout that would make him a virtual invalid had shown signs of restricting his movement and affecting his character. In almost constant, often terrible, pain, he was short tempered, irritable, and seemingly preoccupied. His difficulty walking meant that powerful and proud patricians were required to make the journey to the Medici palace on Via Larga to be received in the manner of a prince. When he did venture out, Piero was carried on a litter reinforcing that image of the head of the Medici family as a potentate, carried like a pope or a pasha. To the fiercely proud and jealous Florentine republican political class this was extremely objectionable. The optics of Piero's manipulation of the republic were discordant, unlike Cosimo's, who always seemed able to sense the mood of the city and its leading citizens and acted accordingly.

Piero's lack of his father's acumen and finely tuned ear to Florentine sensibilities were made evident when he called in loans made by his father to the city's merchants and bankers. The Medici bank was found at the beginning of Piero's regime to be undercapitalized, so Piero chose to call in loans, close certain foreign branches, and restrict lending, all at a time of economic insecurity in Italy because of the decline in eastern trade and increased competition from northern Europe following the end of the Hundred Years' War. In effect, he chose to sacrifice social and political capital to restore the financial capital of the family bank.

The growing alienation of the political elite from Piero reached a crisis in 1465–1466. The death of Cosimo in 1464 had given hope to those opposed to the Medici that their removal was a real possibility. Several men from very prominent families began to agitate to open the lists of electors and return to more frequent rotation of office and thus weaken the instruments of Medici control. Sensing Piero's weakness and possible exile, ambitious politicians began forming opposing factions, hoping to replace the Medici or at least ensure a level of influence in any recovery of the pristine republic. In the councils of the Signoria, Medici supporters were occasionally reduced to a minority, and it appeared that the machine that Cosimo had built was running out of energy. There is also a popular legend that some conspirators planned to assassinate Piero in August of 1466 by ambushing his cortege as it returned to Florence from the villa of Careggi. According to this story, young Lorenzo de'Medici, Piero's son, led the advance party back to the city but was accosted by thugs asking whether Piero's party was far behind. Sensing an attack, Lorenzo warned his father to take another route. Although often repeated, there is no evidence that this ever happened, but it did add to Lorenzo's reputation for mature, clear thinking and action even as a teenager.

Figure 7. Domenico Ghirlandaio was commissioned by the wealthy
factor in the Medici bank, Francesco Sassetti (1421–1490), to
fresco his family's burial chapel in the church of Santa Trinita
in 1480. The work was finished in 1486. Above, the focus of the
narrative is the granting of the rule to St. Francis, but in effect it is
a Medici group portrait, with an image of Lorenzo de'Medici with
the Sassetti family around him (at right). Emerging from a lower
level is Angelo Poliziano leading his pupils, the sons of Lorenzo
the Magnificent: Piero, Giovanni, and Giuliano. Although the
recognition of the Franciscan Order took place in Rome in the
thirteenth century, the background is the Piazza della Signoria in
the later fifteenth century. (Image via Wikimedia, public domain.)

What saved Piero and the Medici was, to a degree, the memory of
instability in the republic before Cosimo's assumption of control in
1464, and a lack of discipline among the leaders of the anti-Medici factions. It became apparent that they were agitating for their own interests
rather than for the well-being of the republic; consequently, some will-
ingly abandoned their fellows and returned to Medici allegiance when
the odds of their succeeding in overthrowing Piero declined. Addition-
ally the very clear support of Duke Galeazzo Maria Sforza of Milan for
Piero de'Medici (Francesco Sforza had died in early March of 1466)
resulted in the fear of armed intervention on his behalf should there be a
change in regime, and the political classes of Florence became more willing to sustain Medici control, although grudgingly. A stable, secure, and
peaceful city, even if compromised in its liberty and less open to dissent,

was infinitely preferable to war, internal factional competition, and even greater economic uncertainty.

A *Parlamento* was called, bringing into the Piazza della Signoria the citizens of the republic. They agreed to the establishment of a committee (*Balìa*) that exiled the leaders of the anti-Medici factions, reduced the role of lot in the election of officials, and provided unusual protection to the Medici by granting the *podestà* extraordinary authority for five years. These measures were calculated to restore Piero and the Medici supporters to their leading positions in the republic and neutralize the opposition. In the end, the voices of stability, security, caution, and established practice had won out over the widespread discontent with Piero's regime.

Nevertheless, it was fortunate for the Medici family and its party machine that Piero died soon after, at the end of 1469, even if his early death was personally tragic. It is perhaps even more fortunate that his eldest son and heir, then just twenty, was one of the most gifted, charismatic, and remarkable men of the fifteenth century: Lorenzo di Piero de'Medici, known as *Il Magnifico*.

Lorenzo di Piero, Il Magnifico (The Magnificent, 1469–1492)

Early Life

Lorenzo was from childhood a gifted and attractive figure. He enjoyed an excellent education under the humanist priest Gentile Becchi and had the advantage of first observing and then participating in the learned discussions that revolved around that Platonic academy, in the family palace and in the humanist coteries that abounded in Florence in the late 1450s and 1460s. He was very close to his equally remarkable mother, Lucrezia Tornabuoni. She was an accomplished religious poet, astute adviser in all manner of things, including business, and her collaboration with Lorenzo would characterize their relationship for the rest of her life. Lorenzo also had a natural ability as a poet in the vernacular tradition—both in obscene carnival songs and deeply felt religious poetry—and he had a magnetic common touch that separated him so obviously from his father. Furthermore, as a young man he was used as an ambassador and as a kind of master of ceremonies for both his family and the city, giving him easy manners among the powerful and a broad knowledge of Italian affairs. Mature beyond his years, furnished with a splendid mind, and a good humanist education, Lorenzo was almost universally seen as the hope of both Florence and the Medici faction.

Piero had determined not to marry his eldest son in the city, as he himself and his father, Cosimo, had done. Rather, he identified a young girl from the great Roman feudal clan of Orsini, an ancient family that had produced cardinals and *condottieri* for centuries. The reasons for this were many. First, given the complex manner in which the Medici were perceived in the city, marrying the third generation of uncrowned rulers into a patrician family could cause jealousy among the others, and there was none equal in status to Lorenzo. Second, Piero hoped that marrying well away from Tuscany might reduce the possibility of Lorenzo's children inheriting the family disease of gout. Third, Piero was beginning to see the Medici as a dynasty, so forging an alliance with a clan that controlled vast estates in Lazio and enjoyed very close links to the papacy would be well received, at least outside of Florence. Finally, the Orsini were *condottieri*, with a large and skilled mercenary army; given the unsettled nature of Florentine politics after 1464, this might well be useful and worth risking the obvious distaste with which the still republican elite in the city would view such a union.

Lucrezia Tornabuoni largely made the match, and her description of the teenaged Clarice Orsini written after meeting the girl in Rome is enlightening. Clarice is described physically, with some mention of her clothes, but little about her intellectual or cultural interests. Despite her adulation of her son, Lorenzo's mother saw Clarice as the healthy and well-formed young girl who would secure the dynasty through delivering many equally healthy children. In fact, Clarice and Lorenzo had absolutely nothing in common. She had only the most perfunctory education and was raised like a Roman noblewoman to be withdrawn and without curiosity. She had no visible knowledge of or interest in art, philosophy, poetry, or music. She was pious and expected to be obedient, and to a degree, invisible. When she was brought to Florence, there was little rejoicing, except for the required feasts and entertainments. That said, she did provide Lorenzo with ten children before her own early death at just forty, and the match was seen as sufficiently successful and useful that Lorenzo arranged for his own eldest son, Piero di Lorenzo, to marry a girl from that same Orsini clan.

The nature of Florentine—indeed Renaissance—customs was visible in the knightly entertainment arranged for the betrothal of Lorenzo and Clarice. The main public event was a joust in the chivalric tradition, redolent with the symbols of medieval courtly love. Although now betrothed to marry Clarice, Lorenzo's object of love in the tournament was the beautiful Lucrezia Donati, whose favor he wore and whose love he pretended to seek. It has been suggested that she was his mistress, but the evidence is ambiguous at best. Lucrezia's husband was indeed sent away on a diplomatic mission, but his rank would lead to such appointments regardless. In fact, there is little absolute proof that Lorenzo took mistresses. His name was associated with several well-born women, but the nature of the relationships was unclear. And, the most telling detail is that he produced no illegitimate children. Even the bourgeois and high-minded Cosimo had had a natural son, Carlo (who became a distinguished prelate), and Lorenzo's younger brother Giuliano left one of his mistresses pregnant at the time of his death, a boy who would become Pope Clement VII.

The Death of Piero and the Accession of Lorenzo (1469)

Clarice and Lorenzo were married in Florence in June of 1468, a symbol that he had entered full maturity, a recognition that led to a series of diplomatic missions later that year. Then in December of the following year, Piero di Cosimo de'Medici was dead, leaving the twenty-year-old Lorenzo the head of Medici party machine and de facto the most powerful man in Florence. He wrote at the time that he assented to the entreaties of the leaders of the city to assume the role his father and grandfather had played and he, for the good of the city, reluctantly agreed, despite his youth. This often-repeated statement is of course ingenuous. He knew what was to come and prepared for his inheritance of power by negotiating for the support of Galeazzo Maria Sforza of Milan and with the *capi* of the Medici faction at home. These loyal and skilled politicians took advantage of the popularity of young Lorenzo and the fear of renewed instability among the ruling elite to reinforce Medici control. Important constitutional changes were enacted that seemed insignificant but in reality guaranteed greater Medici control of elected officials and the political agenda. The *accoppiatori* were to be chosen by their predecessors and the priors then in office, reducing the threat of the election of an unfavorable Signoria. They enlarged the Council of One Hundred, established by Cosimo, by adding a committee whose composition would surely be loyal Medici supporters; the other two old councils of the Commune and the People lost the right to approve taxation, military, and electoral policies. Lorenzo, as a consequence, enjoyed from the beginning of his mandate a remarkable degree of authority, provided he could work closely with those seasoned politicians who acted in his name.

The Sack of Volterra (1472)

Lorenzo also learned the cruel lesson of power when the subject town of Volterra revolted in 1472 over control of its alum mines. Alum was a precious and scarce commodity in Italy and particularly important to Florence, as it was used in the cleansing of raw wool and for fixing the colors of dye in cloth. The mining of alum and its distribution was managed by a private company in which Lorenzo held an interest; the Volterrans felt they were not receiving sufficient return from their valuable commodity, so they seized the mine and humiliated the company by killing two Volterran investors aligned with the Medici. And, they gathered soldiers to defend the city against Florence under whose rule Volterra had chafed in the past. Seeing his opponents in Florence using this crisis to undermine his still untested authority, fearing the example of a revolt of subject towns in support of Volterra, realizing the importance of alum to the Florentine textile industry, and having a personal interest in the profits of the company, Lorenzo engaged the mercenary army of Duke Federigo da Montefeltro of Urbino to besiege the town. After twenty-five days, the city capitulated, but a brawl among soldiers led to the army looting the city mercilessly, following a riot of murder, rape, destruction, and plunder. Lorenzo was obviously personally distressed by the news of this event as he went immediately to Volterra to distribute assistance, much from his own pocket, and promised that amends would be made; however, he honored the duke of Urbino and took credit for forceful and decisive action. While some of his own supporters and family urged caution and flexibility in the Volterra crisis, Lorenzo must have made the final and fateful decision to use force. He was still young and saw the situation as a threat to his authority, faction, and family. As a man he was likely appalled by the violence; as a young and untested political boss he believed it was necessary.

Figure 8. The painted terracotta bust of Lorenzo de'Medici by Verrocchio (Andrea di Michele di Francesco de' Cioni, c. 1435–1488) is probably one of the most accurate likenesses of Lorenzo from the time of the Pazzi Conspiracy. It is believed to be the model from which votive wax images of Lorenzo were fashioned in thanksgiving for his surviving the assassination attempt. One of these was dressed in the very clothes Lorenzo wore when attacked. (Image via Wikimedia, public domain.)

The Pazzi Conspiracy (1478)

Of all the events in the story of the Medici in Florence none attracts stronger emotion than the Pazzi Conspiracy. The roots of the intrigue lay deep in the complex relationship between Florence and the Papal States on its eastern frontier. A great many regimes in Florence had supported the virtual independence of the petty tyrants who ruled the small cities and territories in the Romagna ostensibly as papal vicars. Florence feared a more centralized and aggressive papacy in these territories and consequently provided assistance and diplomatic support to ensure some measure of fragmentation in the States of the Church.

The election of Francesco della Rovere as Pope Sixtus IV in 1471 added to these tensions. He was among the most nepotistic successors of St. Peter in the history of the Church, and he wished to provide for his many della Rovere and Riario nephews through senior appointments in the Church or as rulers of principalities dependent on the Holy See. The city of Imola, close to the Florentine frontier, was the flash point. The ruler of Imola, Taddeo Manfredi, wished to sell the town, and the duke of Milan agreed to purchase it for 40,000 ducats. This would be a transfer of authority in reality to Lorenzo who wanted to control Imola to ensure Florentine security. Pope Sixtus, however, intervened and instructed Duke Galeazzo Maria to transfer it to the papacy so that he might install his nephew Girolamo Riario as its ruler. Sixtus then instructed Lorenzo to lend him the payment for the city, as was appropriate as the pope's banker. Lorenzo refused, citing insufficient funds—which might have been true—and advised the other large Florentine bank in Rome, that of the Pazzi family, to refuse as well.

The relations between the Pazzi and the Medici were complicated. The Pazzi were an ancient magnate family whose name (*pazzi* means "crazy" in Italian) stems from their heroics in the first Crusade in 1099. As magnates they were initially barred from office after the Ordinances of Justice (1293), but they were slowly rehabilitated under Cosimo so that they might take part in civic affairs and operate their bank more effectively. Despite some close ties to the Medici, the Pazzi considered them upstarts and resented their position as the leading family in the city, a role the Pazzi believed they themselves should aspire to achieve. As a consequence, the Pazzi not only gave the pope the money needed to acquire Imola but also revealed the pressure Lorenzo had put on them not to do so. Through this, the Medici lost the papal account and gained the hatred of both Pope Sixtus IV and his nephew Girolamo Riario.

Lorenzo himself proved vindictive, thus adding to the Pazzi's resentment against Lorenzo. He arranged for a law to be passed in 1476 that gave male nephews preference over daughters in inheritances where there was no will. This legislation was obviously directed against the Pazzi, one of whom had married a woman who expected a large bequest under traditional procedures but was instead passed over because the law was retroactive. The head of the family, Jacopo de'Pazzi, was so incensed that he fell in with those in Rome who believed that the Medici had to be eliminated.

It is likely, however, that the conspiracy was planned in Rome. Pope Sixtus' hatred of Lorenzo was fueled by issues of ecclesiastical preferment, as well as personal and clan hostility. Lorenzo had objected to the papal appointment of Francesco Salviati-Riario as archbishop of Florence. Salviati was related to the pope's nephew Girolamo Riario and was a close supporter of Sixtus himself, so Lorenzo objected to a known enemy being named to control the Church in Florence. Although Lorenzo successfully blocked Salviati's elevation, Sixtus retaliated by appointing him archbishop of Pisa. Again, Lorenzo objected but he could not stop it, so he refused to permit Salviati to travel to Pisa to assume his see.

As early as 1475 there were suspicions in Rome that Girolamo Riario, Jacopo de'Pazzi, and Archbishop Salviati were organizing a conspiracy with the blessing of the pope, although he disingenuously remarked how he wanted to avoid bloodshed. News of the plot was gathered by the efficient intelligence network of the duke of Milan, which was then passed along to Lorenzo. Lorenzo, however, seems to have discounted the information because little was done to change his pattern of life; but by 1477 it was widely believed that there was a conspiracy against him, although there was not much he could do without more information.

By April of 1478 the plot had advanced to the point that it was necessary to strike. In 1476 Lorenzo's partner in Italian affairs, Duke Galeazzo Sforza of Milan, had been assassinated in church on the day after Christmas, and this seemed to foreshadow the plot against Lorenzo and give the conspirators much hope. Furthermore, Lorenzo's popularity among the political classes seemed to have declined somewhat because of his use of non-Florentines as officials and close confidants, especially Piero Dovizi da Bibbiena, who served as his private secretary, and his brother who functioned as Lorenzo's personal representative abroad. This was perceived as more the actions of a prince than a republican magistrate who should have drawn on Florentine patricians for important positions.

On Sunday, April 26, the decision was to murder Lorenzo and his brother Giuliano in the cathedral at Mass. There was last-minute defection from the plot when the soldier hired to kill Lorenzo refused to commit murder in a church, particularly when the signal to strike was the ringing of the bell at the Elevation of the Host. In his place were suborned two priests, one from Volterra, who hated Lorenzo because of the sack of the city. Ironically, in the margins of the plot was Federigo, duke of Urbino, whose army had committed the outrage on the city. Young men of the Pazzi family and their co-conspirators were to accompany Giuliano to ensure he attended Mass, as he had been unwell, and to ensure that he was not armed. At the appointed hour the conspirators struck. Giuliano was killed almost immediately but Lorenzo was only wounded in the neck, indicating the priests' lack of skill with a dagger. He was wrapped in a heavy cloak and brought to the cathedral sacristy where the door was barred and his wound sucked in case the dagger had been poisoned. Soon after in the resulting chaos Lorenzo and his supporters returned to the Medici palace to gather their forces.

Simultaneously, Francesco Salviati, the archbishop of Pisa, no longer dressed in his full episcopal regalia, went to the Palazzo della Signoria and demanded entry. He and his party were instructed to kill the pro-Medici priors and secure the palace. However, the Signoria sensed a plot

Figure 9. The Cathedral of Florence, Santa Maria del Fiore, where the violent events of the Pazzi Conspiracy occurred. The church was designed by Arnolfo di Cambio beginning in 1296, in the period after the creation of the Guild Republic following the Ordinances of Justice. The bell tower (*campanile*) was the work of Giotto (1334, but not complete at his death in 1337). The wonderful dome, designed by Filippo Brunelleschi, was constructed between 1420 and 1436. The façade is nineteenth century. (Image via Wikimedia, CC-BY SA 4.0 license.)

and Salviati was locked in the palace; and once the word of Giuliano's murder and the attempt on Lorenzo's life was received, the archbishop had a rope tied around his neck and was thrown from the window of the Room of the Two Hundred, his body hanging against the palace walls for the city to see.

Jacopo de'Pazzi had the role of rallying the city in support of the coup. He rode into the Piazza della Signoria with some others, all shouting "Liberty and the People" (*Popolo e Libertà*). By now, however, the entire city knew of the events in the cathedral and the body of the archbishop was visible on the walls of the palace. Rather than join the conspiracy, the population—and not just traditional Medici clients—responded to Pazzi with "*Palle, Palle*" (literally "Balls," that is, the symbols on the Medici coat of arms and the rallying cry of their faction). A frenzy of murder and looting ensued, with members of the Pazzi family and anyone suspected of collusion with them torn to pieces by the mob. Their houses were sacked and burned, and even their innocent kin hunted down. Because it was now certain that the plot had failed and that Lorenzo was alive, the entire city rallied to the Medici, with no one wanting even to be suspected of any sympathy for the assassins. As many as seventy-five people died that day, although some conspirators escaped; but even these were traced and returned to Florence for execution. The Pazzi family property was confiscated, and their very name was to be obliterated in a classic example of *damnatio memoriae*. For a long period, Pazzi girls were not permitted to marry to ensure that the line would end. So, in their attempt to expunge the Medici, the Pazzi were the victims of their own conspiracy.

The War of the Pazzi Conspiracy (1478–1480)

The longer-term effects of the failed conspiracy ironically succeeded in cementing Lorenzo and the Medici much more deeply into Florence. This was illustrated most clearly in the response of the city to the War of the Pazzi Conspiracy. Because an archbishop had been killed, Pope Sixtus demanded Lorenzo be surrendered to the Church for justice; of course, the Signoria refused. An interdict was placed on the city, denying its citizens Catholic rites until Lorenzo came to Rome; the city ignored it. The pope required his vassal King Ferrante of Naples, with the cooperation of the *condottiere* duke of Urbino, to declare war on Florence. Ferrante was in a difficult position because he was illegitimate, and according to feudal law, the pope, as his lord, could depose him in favor of one of the other claimants to his throne. Thus, a Papal-Neapolitan army marched into Tuscany and captured a number of important towns between Florence and Siena.

Florence was in fact in a very disadvantaged position. The city had not been prepared for war and its traditional allies were in disarray. Milan was struggling to determine the regency after the assassination of Duke Galeazzo Maria, and Venice was at war with the Turks. There was support from Mantua and Ferrara, but that hardly compensated for the strength of the armies mounted by Naples, Urbino, and the papacy. Still, Florence held fast against the approaching forces of Sixtus IV, despite the expense and the serious nature of the threat.

As the war continued, there began to be mutterings against Lorenzo as the cause of the existential danger the Pazzi Conspiracy had brought on the city. A sympathetic Signoria granted him the right to travel about the city with as many armed retainers as necessary for his protection; and the city—the entire city—mourned the death of Giuliano, who had been a sincerely beloved figure, and one whose *joie de vivre* mitigated Lorenzo's more austere character. Nevertheless, after the late autumn of 1479, Lorenzo knew something dramatic had to be done to ensure the independence of his city and the security of his regime. He sent agents to negotiate with Ferrante's son, the duke of Calabria, who was in command of the papal troops ravaging the Florentine dominion. He also broached through the good offices of the Milanese the idea of treating directly with Ferrante for a separate peace with Naples. In a dramatic address to the Signoria in November of that year, he announced that he intended to go to Naples to negotiate personally with Ferrante. It was a perilous move, despite the reassurances he had received, inasmuch as Ferrante had more to gain from the pope than from Florence. Nevertheless, he left and arrived in Naples, where he would spend almost the next four months at the court of the king whose armies were threatening his city and rule.

It has been suggested that Ferrante drew out the discussions as long as possible in hopes that a popular rebellion in Florence would expel the Medici, leaving Ferrante free to claim victory, and either hand Lorenzo over to Sixtus for almost certain execution or protect him as a kind of hostage for Florentine and papal good will. Moreover, the situation in Florence seemed to indicate that a change of regime was possible because many of the patrician factions were looking for an alternative to Lorenzo, now that he was out of the city, to allow peace to be made and a new man exalted by the popular will to manage the republic. Then a great piece of luck gave Lorenzo the final bargaining chip he needed. In early 1480 the French and their supporters in Italy saw an opportunity to resume that struggle between the House of Aragon and the House of Anjou for the crown of Naples that had characterized the affairs of the *regno* (the kingdom, as Naples was usually called, because it was the only kingdom on the Italian peninsula). Ferrante's insecure tenure on his throne made him realize that some accommodation with Florence, a traditional French ally, was useful, even if it angered the pope. So, armed with something like a peace accord, Lorenzo returned to Florence in March of 1480, claiming victory through his personal diplomacy. His welcome home was enthusiastic, blunting all the dissent that had begun to murmur during his long absence.

Lorenzo and his party knew they had to seize this moment. The fear of insurrection in the city had illustrated that the Medici's hold on power was not certain and could be shaken by events. So, in April, the month after his return, Lorenzo called for a committee (*Balìa*) to be struck to change again the constitution of the city to tighten Medici control. The result was the Council of Seventy, a new body with extraordinary powers. It became the effective executive committee of the Signoria, controlling elections and determining what policies would be forwarded to the other instruments of government. Never before had the republic of Florence been so centralized in one body that became the heart of the new Medicean regime. It was also to hold power for five years, undermining the principle of rotation in office. The Medici were moving toward a much more obviously managed government in ways that Cosimo would not have recognized.

There was another incident that permitted Florence and Lorenzo to escape the still-threatening residual effects of the War of the Pazzi Conspiracy. After all, Neapolitan troops were still in the southern territories of the republic; Pope Sixtus IV was still demanding that Lorenzo go to Rome to beg forgiveness; and Sixtus and Girolamo Riario were still hopeful of driving the Medici from their control of Florence. In the summer of 1480, Mohammed the Conqueror, the Ottoman ruler who had captured Constantinople, attacked and seized the Neapolitan city of Otranto in Puglia, cruelly slaughtering those inhabitants who refused to convert, including those who had sought refuge in the city's cathedral. Otranto was a seaport so the Ottomans were seen to have gained a foothold in Italy. Ferrante was rightly frightened and withdrew his army from Tuscany to relieve Otranto, and the pope was now more afraid of the Turks and in need of Italian unity and support than furious at Lorenzo and the Medici. Ferrante acceded to Lorenzo's diplomacy and the pope softened his position, allowing Florence to send a delegation to Rome to seek absolution for the killing of Archbishop Salviati rather than insisting on Lorenzo himself appearing in Rome as a penitent. Lorenzo had returned home with the best deal possible in March of 1480, but nevertheless one which did not altogether resolve the issues that drove the pope's anger; the following summer Sixtus needed an ally in Florence able to help pay for an assault on the Turks and the security of the Italian peninsula. In effect, Lorenzo, and to a degree Florence, had been absolved by the Turks.

The Rule of Lorenzo, 1480–1492

Lorenzo emerged in the spring of 1480 as a prince in all but name. He was permitted to travel with an armed retinue; he determined policy; and foreign states dealt with him directly rather than through the usual offices of the republic. He began to take substantial amounts of communal money to sustain his style of life, including the acquisition of his collections of rare objects. All significant appointments both in the city and in the subject territories required his approval; he interfered in the judicial process and expected to be consulted in marriage negotiations if the families involved were influential. His personal staff, such as Piero Dovizi da Bibbiena, and his brother Bernardo (who would become a cardinal under Lorenzo's son, Pope Leo X), and Bernardo di Michelozzo, the son of Cosimo's architect, played a more powerful role in the operation of the state than ever before, with Lorenzo according them authority in both domestic and diplomatic spheres; some of these men grew very rich at the expense of the state as well as the Medici. Lesser guildsmen with no personal influence or prestige in the city were given senior positions because their authority came from their loyalty to Lorenzo alone, and those with great patrician lineages were passed over out of fear that their pride, jealousy, or family reputation could attract dissenters. Remembering the personal tragedy and crisis of the Pazzi Conspiracy, Lorenzo did not tolerate serious dissent. Men from some of the most ancient and prominent families in the city were executed for conspiring against him; others were exiled when there were merely rumors of an attempt to organize an opposition to Lorenzo's increasingly personal rule. Florence was being transformed from a managed republic to a clandestine principality.

Patronage and Interests

Lorenzo did not enjoy the same reputation as a patron as did his grandfather, Cosimo. In part, this resulted from the declining income of the bank, which made extremely lavish patronage somewhat more difficult, but it also stemmed from the nature of Lorenzo's interests and his character. He liked being surrounded by profound thinkers, particularly if they had quick wits, and his support of the so-called Platonic academy surrounding Marsilio Ficino at Careggi illustrates this. Men such as Count Giovanni Pico della Mirandola, the aristocratic young poly-math from near Modena, took Florentine Neoplatonism deeply into the realms of the unity of truth and the divine nature of humanity, as well as mysticism and magic. Angelo Poliziano was a very close associate of Lorenzo and a brilliant poet and scholar who continued the traditions of Florentine humanism to the end of the century, while celebrating the lives and loves of the Medici through works such as his *Stanze per la Giostra di Giuliano de'Medici (Stanzas for the Joust of Giuliano de'Medici)*. Luigi Pulci, a satiric poet, with anti-clerical tendencies but a brilliant wit, wrote his mock epic *Morgante Maggiore* in the company of Lorenzo and his circle.

Lorenzo did not commission painting to the degree as his grandfather or even his father. There were specific commissions, especially the fresco cycle for his villa, Lo Spadoletto, near Volterra, that once contained cycles by Sandro Botticelli, Filippo Lippi, the Ghirlandaio, and Pietro Perugino. Sadly, the entire mythological decoration of the villa has been lost, and it is partly for this reason that Lorenzo's reputation for patron-age has suffered. He might have commissioned the famous *Pallas and the Centaur* (c. 1481) from Botticelli to commemorate the events of the War of the Pazzi Conspiracy, but it might also have been ordered by his cousin, Lorenzo di Pierfrancesco, who certainly commissioned Bot-ticelli's famous *Primavera* and *The Birth of Venus* for his villa at Castello. And we know that the young Michelangelo lived at Palazzo Medici for some five years under Lorenzo's direct patronage.

Lorenzo did ensure that his favorite painters found other patrons, often intervening on their behalf. It is thus that Domenico Ghirlandaio likely received the commissions for the Sassetti chapel in Santa Trinita, where a portrait of Lorenzo with the Sassetti family appears. Similarly, the Ghirlandaio workshop painted the chapel of his mother's family, the Tornabuoni, in Santa Maria Novella. In part to reconcile with Pope Sixtus IV after the Pazzi Conspiracy, Lorenzo arranged for Botticelli, Perugino, Ghirlandaio, and Cosimo Rosselli to travel to Rome during 1481–1482 to paint the walls of the pope's new Sistine Chapel, whose vault and altar wall would in the next century be painted by that other Florentine, Michelangelo. Similarly, Lorenzo encouraged Leonardo da Vinci to go to Milan in 1482 to work for Lodovico Sforza, il Moro. Nor did he stand in the way of his favorite sculptor, Verrocchio, whose workshop he patronized in Florence, from casting the bronze equestrian statue of Colleoni in Venice.

It was perhaps architecture that engaged Lorenzo most deeply, however, after literature and philosophy. He commissioned Giuliano da San Gallo to build his beautiful and innovative villa at Poggio a Caiano in 1485, taking a very active and engaged interest in the work. Later, in 1488, that architect was commissioned to build the Augustinian church of San Gallo, just outside the walls of the city, near the now eponymous gate. So involved was Lorenzo and so important was this commission that Giuliano Giamberti came to be known as Giuliano da San Gallo, renamed to a degree by Lorenzo himself, who remarked that he would always be known for this work. Sadly, as with the decoration of Lo Spadoletto, the church is gone, destroyed during the siege of Florence in 1529. Moreover, Lorenzo considered himself an architect—or at least an architectural designer—because he submitted his own plan for the competition to determine the façade of the cathedral. It is likely that it was not overly compelling because the competition was adjourned at Lorenzo's suggestion—and the cathedral consequently was without a complete façade until the late nineteenth century.

The cathedral, and Orsanmichele before it, also benefited from Lorenzo's patronage in a little-recognized manner. He strongly supported the great musician and cathedral organist Antonio Squarcialupi (d. 1480), who was a friend and member of his coterie. Squarcialupi, a native Florentine, was celebrated throughout Italy and his collection of musical manuscripts contributed to the archival richness of the city.

But it was in the collection of rare gems, small ancient objects, and rare cabinet pieces that Lorenzo's connoisseurship achieved brilliance. He had a network of agents around Italy, with connections across Europe, furnished with the brief to acquire the most beautiful and rarest objects for his collection. Many of the ancient pieces Lorenzo had mounted by Florentine goldsmiths, and many were incised "LAVR.MED." to identify them as part of his collection: these are still to be seen in the Museo degli Argenti (Silver Museum) in the Pitti Palace in Florence. Add to these small *objets de vertu* Lorenzo's love of fine manuscripts and a sense of his personal taste emerges. He was a public figure, a prince in all but name, but his own pleasure was in things he could enjoy in private, objects with a tactile quality and which celebrated fine workmanship, rarity, or age. His grandfather had enjoyed making the city beautiful through large public works while Lorenzo saw the cultivation of his own exquisite taste and refinement as perhaps more appropriate for a man in his exalted position. The Medici had really become quasi monarchs.

The Last Years of Lorenzo and the Rise of Savonarola

Lorenzo's last years were a continuation of his policies established after 1480. There remained considerable opposition among the old patrician clans to both the centralized authority Lorenzo exercised and their consequent exclusion from real power. Lorenzo's use of his personal staff in official capacities angered the old families even more, as they feared losing forever their traditional influence over the republic. He also managed to gain a significant foothold in Rome by convincing Pope Innocent VIII to name his second son, Giovanni, a cardinal in 1489, despite his very uncanonical age: thirteen. This elevation, initially made secretly—*in pectore*—was negotiated through Lorenzo's marrying his daughter Maria Maddalena to the pope's son Franceschetto Cybo in 1487. His eldest son, Piero di Lorenzo, he had married to a relation of his wife, an Orsini, but of the Neapolitan branch of that large, feudal clan. This union again connected the Medici to one of Italy's greatest noble families and offered support through their private armies. Although two other daughters married into prominent Florentine patrician families (Salviati and Ridolfi), the optics were that Lorenzo was effecting the kinds of alliances a princely family would make.

It was during the last years of Lorenzo's life that these tensions with the Florentine elite would be exacerbated by a growing dissatisfaction among the poorer, disenfranchised citizens. Lorenzo had tried to sustain his charismatic hold on the *popolo minuto* through the usual Medici instruments of processions, carnival festivities, popular entertainments, and patronage, but the mood of the city had changed. Lorenzo had himself become more distant, separated by his armed retainers and obviously happiest, not among the revelers at carnival any longer, but among his highly cultivated friends in the Platonic academy or in his study surrounded by his collection of rare objects and gems.

It was in this environment that Girolamo Savonarola returned to Florence for his second and last residence in the monastery of San Marco, the institution re-founded by Cosimo de'Medici and rebuilt by Michelozzo. Savonarola was born in Ferrara in 1452, the grandson of an eminent physician. He entered a Dominican monastery in 1475 after completing his arts degree in Ferrara. The Dominicans encouraged him to continue his studies in theology at Bologna, as he was very intelligent and ascetic in his devotional life, and in 1476 he was ordained a priest. In 1482 he was sent to Florence where he was given responsibility for the training of novices in the order. He also preached occasionally but was unsuccessful with his congregations because of both his accent and his lack of rhetorical skill. In a city that respected the elegant use of words, Savonarola appeared as uncultivated, despite his learning. As a result he left Florence and became an itinerant preacher, and it was this experience that changed the focus of his sermons to give voice to an increasingly apocalyptic message, one that better suited the mood of Florence when he returned in 1490.

It is ironic that Savonarola was brought back to San Marco through the intervention of one of Lorenzo's closest friends, Giovanni Pico della Mirandola. Pico himself felt the need for spiritual renewal and, after having heard the Dominican preach, thought him extremely learned in biblical studies and theology, and so would be ideal for Florence. He convinced Lorenzo to support the appointment, despite the serious reservations of the general of the Dominican Order. Moreover, the millenarian perspective of Savonarola was not alien either to Florence or to Italy, even in the age of the Renaissance. There had been a long tradition of mystical, apocalyptic prophecy in Italy from the Middle Ages and Savonarola was within it.

In fact, if any Florentine of the lower classes, and a great many guildsmen and women of all classes, were asked in 1490 who was the greatest of all Florentines, the answer would not be Cosimo de'Medici, and certainly not Brunelleschi or Donatello: it would be Archbishop Antoninus, later to be Sant'Antonino (Antonino Pierozzi, d. 1459, canonized in 1523). He was a Dominican priest, named prior of San Marco a half century before Savonarola, and archbishop of Florence in 1446. Although he accepted the patronage of Cosimo de'Medici—who kept a cell in San Marco—his commitment to helping the poor and desperate was uncompromising. Despite his high office, he lived a very ascetic life, ministering to the poor during periods of plague and helping them after the earthquakes of the 1440s and 1450s. He preached regularly and provided an example of an exemplary life. The population of Florence thought him a saint and gave him the warmly familiar diminutive of his name as an honor, Antonino, as St. Francis had been called *Il Poverello*, the little poor one.

Moreover, preachers, especially famous or emotionally moving speakers, were the rock stars of the age. Sermons were a major form of both entertainment and education for the poor and for women, whose only trips beyond the house were often to church to hear a preacher. Preachers had influence, power, and respect, and they carried the message that those who were suffering, without power or money, without property or employment, would be raised up in the next world or at the time of Christ's return to earth. And, those who tormented the poor, took away their work, left them and their families to starve, treated them with complete disdain, and thought of them as little more than animals would be punished and the retribution would be severe, as befitted a just sentence on those who despised Christ's poor.

Savonarola, then, had an eager audience well prepared for his sermons that prophesied the imminent second coming of Christ, when peace, justice, and love would reign. He built wisely on this and used the rhetorical skill he had now acquired as an itinerant preacher to hammer home a message of hope for the dawn of a new and just era. His sermons soon grew so popular that he had to move to the cathedral, as San Marco proved too small, and his message began to appeal not only to the poor and to women—those outside the political structure of the republic—but also to angry, alienated, and devout patricians who, even if the message seemed not to apply to them, might at least presage the end of Medici control.

Even Lorenzo himself and his immediate coterie felt the power of Savonarola's preaching. Initially, the Dominican did not attack Lorenzo personally, and Lorenzo even protected the monk from charges that some of his statements bordered on the provocative, if not heretical. These had to do with the corruption of the Church and its head, Pope Alexander VI Borgia, and the luxury of prelates and the wealth of a Church that should be devoting its resources—spiritual and material—to the poor. Pico della Mirandola, Sandro Botticelli, and the painter Lorenzo di Credi all fell under Savonarola's influence. Savonarola increasingly attacked the very essence of Florentine humanism, calling it pagan and opposed to true religion. He denounced classical studies and erotic literature and art, and he suggested that these things would interfere with Christ's return.

In the spring of 1492 it was obvious Lorenzo was dying. He had been ill for some time, and his death was likely hastened by the ministrations of his doctors. On his deathbed in April of that year, according to legend, he called for Savonarola to administer extreme unction, as was traditional for the prior of the Medici convent of San Marco. In hearing Lorenzo's confession, Savonarola asked if he repented all of his sins, including having stolen the liberty of his city. In response Lorenzo turned his head to the wall, so absolution was not given. Although there is no evidence for this bit of theater, it does reflect the reality of the situation by 1492; Savonarola was directing his sermons not only against the pope and a corrupt Church or the unfeeling rich, he was also targeting the Medici and their regime.

The Short Regime of Piero di Lorenzo (1492–1494)

Lorenzo's eldest son, Piero, was just twenty when his father died, the same age Lorenzo had been when he assumed direction of the Medici faction in 1469. There the similarity ends. Whereas Lorenzo was already a sophisticated thinker with a grasp of both Florentine and foreign issues, Piero was far less gifted and suffered from a deep insecurity, almost paranoia, which manifested itself in an arrogant, stilted, and distrustful nature. He was also not very intelligent, despite his excellent education. His youth had been characterized by brawling and bragging, which his father and his supporters managed to conceal to some degree. Lorenzo's famous line about his son being a fool was an astute judgment; nevertheless, Medici practice, dynastic pride, and universal expectation meant that there was no attempt to restrict his ascent to power. And there was not really any alternative; his younger brother Giovanni had already been named a cardinal and his future lay in Rome; his youngest brother, Giuliano, was only thirteen at the time of his father's death. Consequently, in a seamless transition of power, Piero was confirmed in all of his father's offices and the powerful members of his faction gathered at the palace in Via Larga to begin the new regime.

It soon became apparent exactly how limited Piero was. His distrustful nature alienated him from a great many of his father's supporters and even members of his own family. His princely arrogance—really a sign of his own fear and insecurity—further angered the old republican patrician families who saw the roots of a monarchy developing. Any advice that counseled accommodation with the old elite or wide cultivation of the less-privileged citizens Piero interpreted as a threat. He saw conspiracies everywhere, which resulted in his closing his circle of advisers and officials to a small group dependent completely on him, restricting his administration to those who expected favors and honors. He raised personal servants and insignificant guildsmen to important positions, thereby driving a deeper wedge between the Medici and the great patrician clans who increasingly believed that he was forming the foundation for a monarchical state.

When news that the French king, Charles VIII, planned to cross the Alps into Italy to claim the crown of Naples reached Italy in 1493, every Italian state looked for ways to deal with the impending crisis. The Medici's once solid connection with Milan was challenged when the regent, Lodovico il Moro, welcomed the invasion as a way to ensure that the legitimate duke, his nephew, who was married to a Neapolitan princess, would not have his father-in-law's military support to oust him and claim his rightful throne. Piero, despite his family's traditional French sympathies, stood apart from the demands of the French, even though he understood that Charles' huge army would have to pass through Florentine territory en route to Naples. Not only did Piero underestimate the danger, he was also heavily influenced by his wife's family, the Orsini of the Neapolitan branch of the clan. His only policy seemed to be temporizing, which alienated everyone.

His position in Florence was further undermined by the ever-growing influence of Savonarola. The Dominican had begun to preach that Charles VIII was God's instrument, sent to cleanse Italy and the Church, a scourge that was required to expunge the sinfulness of Italy and silence the paganism, pride, and luxury Savonarola described as a sordid affront to God. Charles became the new Charlemagne or the new Cyrus; he was a divine messenger who would purify the Church, create a godly people, lead a Crusade that would liberate the Holy Land, and prepare the way for the second coming of Christ. Although the poor, women, and some lesser guildsmen fervently accepted this millenarian prophecy, a number of powerful patricians saw an opportunity to rid Florence of the Medici and use Savonarola as a popular figure to unify the city. Increasingly, open talk of ending the Medici hegemony began to spread among all classes of citizens, but most dangerously for Piero, within the republican elite. Such talk was even heard in the councils of the republic and the Signoria. It was becoming more and more obvious that the Medici regime was unraveling and its loyal adherents were defecting daily.

It was fear of this internal threat more than fear of the French army then marching toward Tuscany that drove Piero to attempt to emulate his father's courageous diplomatic tour de force and travel to the camp of the French king to negotiate a deal to protect Florence and win back popular and patrician support, or at least acceptance, as had happened in 1480. But what the canny, intelligent, and well-prepared Lorenzo managed to achieve with Ferrante of Naples was not a possibility for Piero, nor were the situations in any way parallel. Ferrante was fighting the pope's war, not his; Lorenzo could show the degree to which Neapolitan sovereignty would be reinforced by having a powerful Florence to balance the ambitions of Sixtus IV and the Riario; and, finally, as we have seen, Lorenzo had luck on his side. Piero had little to bargain with, was not at all clever or insightful, and could not be certain of support within the city, as there was increasing talk of welcoming the French into Florence as liberators, releasing the republic from the tyranny of the Medici. And, finally, he deserved his historical descriptor of Piero *Lo Sfortunato*: Piero the Unlucky.

When Piero arrived at the French camp at the end of October 1494 with just a few retainers, he showed just how incompetent and craven he was. He immediately yielded to all of the French demands, and these were exceptional: Florence had to turn over its perimeter fortresses to the French and give the port of Pisa, as well as Livorno, to Charles. Pisa, which had finally been added to the Florentine dominion in 1406, was Florence's seaport, its lifeline to seaborne trade and hope for revitalization in the new world of shifting economic fortunes. Lorenzo had honored the city by making it the seat of the Florentine university, drained the malarial marshes—at least as much as was then possible—and hoped to bring the once proud republic firmly into Florence's growing territorial state. Now it was lost. All Piero received was Charles' promise to support his rule and recognize an alliance with Florence.

The reaction in Florence to this complete, humiliating capitulation on the part of Piero was fury and despair—fury because Piero had acted without any authority to negotiate with the French and had not discussed his cowardly agreement with the Signoria before signing, and despair because Charles demanded an entry into the city with his army, in the manner of a conqueror. Although Piero's few supporters attempted to secure an ex post facto approval of the terms won by the French, no one was in any mood to exonerate Piero's actions or yield to the French. Unfortunately, the French army was already in place, exacting its terms, and Charles VIII was preparing for his entry into Florence, a symbol of the city's humiliation. Piero returned to Florence on November 8 but was met with open hostility. His retinue was pelted with mud and he was treated with disdain. There was an abortive attempt to mount a military defense by calling upon one of his Orsini relations to come with his mercenary army while peasants from Medici estates were marshaled and armed. But it was too late and pointless; the entire city had turned against Piero. The once loyal factional leaders in the Signoria denounced him and some members of his family were attacked, and one killed. Seeing the danger and a coward by nature, Piero fled Florence with his family; bounties were offered for their return, dead or alive, and the Palazzo Medici was seized and looted. Medici servants fled or were tried, and in one case executed. Thus, exactly sixty years after the triumphal return of Cosimo de'Medici to Florence in 1434, the Medici were expelled once more.

CHAPTER THREE
SAVONAROLA AND FLORENCE, THE
NEW JERUSALEM (1494–1498)

Florence without the Medici

The expulsion of the Medici and the disintegration of their faction resulted in a dangerous power vacuum and a divided city. Although few would declare publicly for the Medici, there were those whose careers had grown through the Medici's patronage: these loyalists were encouraged by King Charles VIII's reiteration of his demand that Piero be restored. They were relatively few in number, however, and their party had been reduced by the exile or flight of those who had been closest to Piero. Then there were the great patrician clans whose influence had diminished under Lorenzo and Piero. Many of these wealthy and proud men saw an opportunity to return to a form of oligarchic government in which they, the natural leaders of the republic, would play a privileged leading role. Beneath them were the supporters of a more open, broadly based regime, such as the one that had emerged after the crises of the 1340s. The year 1494 was also a time of crisis, so a united political class of all eligible citizens appealed to them as a way of expunging the "tyranny" of the Medici. With the French about to enter the city and Florence's sovereignty in the balance, the one person who had credibility with a great many Florentines and with the French king was Savonarola.

Savonarola had already been sent to Charles following the discovery of what Piero had yielded to the French. The pious French king was sympathetic to the Dominican because he believed, as did Savonarola, that he was on a divine mission and that he was the new Charlemagne. Nevertheless, Charles still demanded a triumphal entry into the city, although Savonarola tried to convince him of the need to consider Florentine sensibilities. In Florence, Savonarola's counsel held great weight, and at this point he was shrewd in what he advocated. He proposed a policy

of reconciliation with former supporters of the Medici and more negotiations with Charles. So, when Charles did enter Florence on November
17, he did so with only part of his army; still, the sight of 10,000 armed
men marching like conquerors into the city appalled the Florentines.
Furthermore, Charles had abandoned Pisa, resulting in its declaring
independence from Florence, as he felt no need to return it to Florentine
control, and the perimeter fortresses were still held by French garrisons.
Established in the now-vacated Palazzo Medici, Charles demanded that
Florence accept French control, like a captured city, and commit to
a French alliance. A French army was to be garrisoned in the city and
preparations for billeting were well under way. Charles was treating
Florence like a subject territory, conquered in war. Finally, and to a degree
most painful to the Florentines, especially the political classes, Charles
demanded that Piero be restored as the governor of Florence, fulfilling
his pledge to him when they had met at the end of October.

This demand the Signoria absolutely refused, so tensions with the
French were high. It was then that the famous exchange between Charles
and Piero Capponi occurred. Exasperated by the endless negotiations,
Charles stated that to get his way all he had to do was blow upon his
trumpets, to which Capponi replied, "Sire, if you blow upon your trumpets we shall ring upon our bells." Florence, that is, would fight the French
in defense of its liberty. Florence was hardly Charles' purpose in invading
Italy: he sought the crown of Naples. Consequently, after another set of
negotiations, again with Savonarola's deep involvement, a new arrangement was reached. Florence would remain an ally of the French; France
recognized Pisa as Florentine territory but would not help to recapture
the city; the demand to restore Piero was dropped—although Charles
still strongly advised it—and Florence would pay an indemnity of
120,000 florins to the king for his trouble. In many ways it was another
humiliation for Florence, but when the king and his enormous army left
the city on November 28, 1494, Florence was again free to determine its
post-Medici future. And the city had escaped having to hold a French
garrison or be sacked, as happened in other, less fortunate, towns.

The Medici were gone, but they had now to be replaced. The power
vacuum that emerged created a number of mutually exclusive factions
all attempting to benefit from the situation. The old aristocratic clans
expected to be able to manipulate the government through their natural
prestige, experience, and sense of entitlement. Many of those who had
been close to Lorenzo de'Medici abandoned any thought of the Medici's

Figure 10. Francesco Granacci (1469–1543) painted this
scene of the 1494 entry of the French king, Charles VIII, into
Florence in 1527. (Image via Wikimedia, public domain.)

return and indeed had participated in the expulsion of Piero, recogniz-
ing that he would never be able to maintain a grip on power. Even those
opposed to the Medici made common cause with these former *Palleschi*
(Medici supporters, so named from the *palle* or balls on the family's coat of
arms) in order to keep real authority among the patricians, despite some
personal antagonisms, which remained just below the surface. But the
broader base of the politically eligible citizens had no intention of yielding
up their victory to the patricians. The immediate response to the end of
the Medici hegemony had been to abolish their means of control, especially the Council of One Hundred and the Council of Seventy. A *Parlamento* was called and the consequence of this seemed to indicate a much
more widely participatory regime in which almost any adult male citizen
eligible for office might be chosen for the highest positions in the state.

Savonarola and the Great Council

At this point Savonarola enters the political debate. The friar had been
already identified as a natural leader of the Florentine people through

his inclusion in the delegation that brought better terms for Florence from Charles VIII, and he had been steadfast in counseling Charles to leave the city quickly and unmolested in order to fulfill his divine mission in Rome and Naples. Moreover, he was a known anti-Medicean whose very presence would foreclose any attempt by Piero's supporters to allow the Medici's return. Significantly, Savonarola's sermons, although against general political vices and Medici domination, had not yet indicated a serious interest in the political process itself. Furthermore, he was a foreigner and a priest, both of which excluded him from an active political role. Consequently, although many patricians still distrusted him because of his championing of the poor and disadvantaged, in this tense time Savonarola's entry into the constitutional discussions appeared natural and reasonable, even if his ambiguous position in the city added yet another layer of uncertainty and potential social division.

The friar to a degree compounded this instability by preaching to an assembly of male citizens and officials, expressing his admiration for the Venetian constitution which he said obviously was the work of God, as illustrated by its longevity, its popular base in the *Maggior Consiglio* (Great Council), and its stability, even in troubled times. It must be noted that this praise of Venice was not unique to Savonarola: it had been part of Florentine political discourse for a long time. Poggio Bracciolini, who rose to become chancellor of the republic from 1453 to 1458, wrote a praise of the Venetian constitution and spoke for many humanists who saw it as the ideal form of government. There is also a probability that Savonarola hoped that the establishment of a Great Council in Florence would be an instrument of social cohesion in which all citizens might participate and consequently reduce the likelihood of a return to oligarchy or the Medici.

When the various committees responsible for drafting a new constitution for Florence finally reported, the model of a huge council was adopted at the very end of 1494. Its membership was extremely broad as entry was determined by a family having been eligible for public office for at least three generations. The potential list of members numbered well over 3,000, a throng that the patricians knew they could not control so they agitated against it. Equally, however, it was an attractive vehicle to ensure that lists of candidates for high office or tax assessments could not be easily manipulated, securing a fairer and more equitable republic because the council was to enjoy substantial authority over taxation, elections, and policy. To hold such a large group a new space had to be constructed in

HIERONYMI·FERRARIENSIS·A·DEO·
MISSI·PROPHETÆ·EFFIGIES·

Figure 11. This portrait of Girolamo Savonarola was painted by his fellow Dominican, Fra Bartolommeo (1472–1517), in 1498. Bartolommeo (Baccio della Porta) fell under the influence of Savonarola in Florence in the 1490s, eventually entering San Marco as a Dominican friar himself in 1500. (Image via Wikimedia, public domain.)

the Palazzo della Signoria. By early 1496 it was ready to welcome the first iteration of the Great Council.

The Prophetic Tradition in Florence

Savonarola had preached in favor of such a council, and his sermons were now taking a more political as well as apocalyptic tone. To understand how these gloomy messages of a wrathful God and his divine plan to cleanse the Church and prepare for the Second Coming reverberated in Florence just a few years after the death of Lorenzo the Magnificent is to remember the place of prophecy in Italian political culture, the social gospel of the mendicant orders, and, ironically, the humanist praise of Florentine exceptionalism present in civic discourse from at least the time of Leonardo Bruni (chancellor 1427–1444).

For example, the Calabrian abbot, Joachim (Giocchino) of Fiore (d. 1202), looked for prophetic messages in the Book of Revelation to establish a taxonomy of God's plan. His Three Ages were first, the Age of the Father (the Old Testament), second, the Age of the Son (the New Testament), and finally, the Age of the Holy Spirit; this last would begin with a cleansing of the Church, which would no longer need an earthly structure as it would be directed by the order of the just with direct knowledge of Christ. A time of complete freedom and pure religion in an ideal community would emerge, engendering the peace and joy that would result from living in accordance with God's wishes. These Joachimite prophecies were part of the arsenal of itinerant preachers who spread these kinds of ideas throughout Italy, and Savonarola would certainly have heard many versions of these chiliastic interpretations of divine intentions. And Joachim was well known in Florence; Dante, for example, refers to Joachim in the *Commedia*, placing him in Paradise—a clear indication of sympathy with his message.

Similarly, the most ascetic and provocative among the Spiritual Franciscans, the *Fraticelli*, those followers of St. Francis of Assisi who remained true to his repudiation of property and the world, wandered the peninsula. They preached against wealth, luxury, pride, and arrogance—both secular and ecclesiastical—calling for an exaltation of the poor and describing in often chilling detail Christ's just anger against those who have too much at the expense of those with little or nothing. Although the sect was declared heretical in 1296, it continued to have some significant influence, and its preaching among the poor in towns and cities angered and frightened those who governed, often the objects of the *Fraticelli's* angry sermons. This was especially true in Florence where the social disruption feared from their agitation among the Ciompi caused the communal government to banish the sect from the city in 1415; in the late 1420s a number of *Fraticelli* were burned in the city with the full approval of the pope. Although banned and persecuted, the sect survived and went underground and its message to the poor endured: before the wrath of God, the rich and powerful should tremble because a terrible judgment would soon be at hand.

All of these prophetic traditions gave Savonarola's religious message a deep resonance of familiarity, reinforcing the power of his message, already exalted by his foretelling of the French invasions and the deaths of both Lorenzo and Pope Innocent VIII in 1492. However, the secular traditions of civic humanism added a great deal to the acceptance of the friar's message as well. Leonardo Bruni in particular, that great humanist chancellor, scholar, and historian, had in his *History of Florence* and his *Praise of the City of Florence* lauded Florentine exceptionalism. The republic was the guarantor of republican freedom in Italy, and it had a mission to sustain it at home and protect it outside its own territory. Florence had freedom and a unique mission incorporated into its DNA, cemented by its history of standing firm against all tyrants. It was a product of its heroic destiny, and the city was the New Athens or the New Rome. It was preeminent among the Italian states in its virtue, power, and beauty: it was an example and a beacon for others to emulate.

This Florentine republican propaganda and ideology of exceptionalism and its destiny to become the New Rome equally fed into Savonarola's preaching. It is a small adjustment to translate the New Athens or Rome into the New Jerusalem, and its civic destiny and exceptionalism into the fulfillment of Christian millenarianism. Florence, in Savonarola's view, was not chosen by its virtue and history as much as by its faith and fervor in the completion of the divine plan. It was to be the instrument of renewal for the Church and the place of the Second Coming, once it was cleansed of its addiction to pagan ideas, books, art, and learning, which were to be replaced by things seen as pleasing to God.

This message reached a very sympathetic audience. The expulsion of the Medici had resulted in a rejection to a degree of the dominant "court" culture under Lorenzo, especially the very recondite ideas of Florentine Neoplatonism and "pagan" humanism. Although anticlericalism had long been a tradition in the city, as the tales of Boccaccio reveal, the *Morgante Maggiore* of Luigi Pulci and the pagan inspiration in the poetry of Poliziano went further than a little popular amusement at the expense of lubricious or greedy priests and monks. This literature and art reflected the interests of those closest to the center of power, that is, Lorenzo de'Medici and his friends. To those still proud of the Florentine traditions of bourgeois republican sobriety and simple Christian belief, the carnival songs seemed somewhat more obscene than usual. The memory of Plato's birthday (November 7) being treated as a virtual holy day of obligation at the villa of Careggi, with prayers to St. Socrates to intercede for penitent philosophers, might have just been a bit of pompous theater; but to those with traditional Christian piety and little sense of irony, they were toxic. Furthermore, the ideas that animated Lorenzo's coterie and informed the art of Botticelli, the poetry of Poliziano, and the thought of Pico della Mirandola or Ficino were not easily grasped. These things required years of study, reading, knowledge of Latin at least and ideally Greek, and a desire and the leisure to acquire such things.

Most Florentines, even the most privileged, had little interest in them and consequently felt alienated, left out of the dominant "court" culture of the Medici. This resulted in a sense of exclusion and hence anger. To reject this culture would not be the consequence of ignorance as much as an affirmation of traditional Christian and solid, bourgeois, austere, mercantile Florentine values. The Italian saying "*I fiorentini sono sempre in bottega*" (Florentines are always at work) reflected not only the perception of the city from without but also the self-identified character of its citizens: they were always laboring in their counting houses or banks, not discussing Plato; they were hard-headed, practical men who were also devout Christians. Their model of behavior was not Plato but Sant'Antonino, their revered and saintly late archbishop. Citizens of all classes not only attended Mass but also joined lay confraternities to encourage God to benefit their city through good works, donations, prayers, processions, and hymns. There were the *laudesi* who praised God by singing his praises, and those who comforted the sick and dying or condemned prisoners. Religious art and theater were everywhere and none doubted the articles of faith.

Savonarola's preaching brought these sincere Christians back to their simple faith and republican civic duty and gave them reason to reject— even despise—the culture of privilege and exclusion that characterized the coteries around Lorenzo. The Medici were now gone, so Florence could revert back to what it really was: a Christian, burgher republic whose complexion was not the rarified circle of the Medici, but an older and deeper religious and civic life that they had subverted. The genius of Savonarola was to unite the piety of Florentines with their republican political traditions, welding them into an ideology of spiritual and political reformation.

Savonarola's preaching had become somewhat amorphously political even before the death of Lorenzo inasmuch as he preached against not only moral but also political and economic sins, demanding penitence and reform from the citizens of his chosen city. In return, he promised not just the divine rewards that come from a purer life but greater wealth and power as a collective reward from God for the city's rehabilitation. And it was as a consequence of these sermons that the reconstituted republic established at the end of 1494 was infused with his Christian principles and a sense of divine destiny.

Piagnoni **and** Arrabbiati

It was, however, not a destiny all accepted. Certainly, many powerful patricians with seats in the Great Council rallied to his message, creating a faction that subscribed to no single class, neighborhood, or clan allegiance: their bond was a commitment to Savonarola's message. These were the *Piagnoni*, or Snivellers, so called from their tendency to weep during the friar's sermons. They were, however, not without opposition. There were others who had no interest in connecting millenarian prophecy with politics or who resented not being able to restore an oligarchic regime when the Medici were expelled. Also, there were young patricians who bristled under the new moral order that forbade gambling, public celebrations not religious in nature, and the closing of the brothels. Then there were those associated with the Franciscans, the other still-powerful mendicant order that resented being upstaged by this Dominican. Moreover, there were those who feared Savonarola's attacks on the ecclesiastical establishment and the papacy. Often these opponents had business connections to Rome or felt that their prospects could be limited by a papal counterattack; or, they were sincere Catholics who accepted the hierarchy of the Church as divinely ordained, despite Savonarola's challenges. Finally, there was an inchoate but substantial group of patricians who resented being called usurers, oppressors of the poor, and, hence, by Savonarola's definition, sinful. Many of these men also saw the fervor with which the disenfranchised Florentines—those without property or resources and the women of the city—supported the friar and his message. It looked too much like a call for a revolution of the kind represented by the Ciompi Revolt of 1378, another time when Florence was opposed to the papacy and suffered under an interdict and loss of trade. This faction opposed to Savonarola was described in equally insulting terms as the *Arrabbiati*, which means either "The Angry" or "The Rabid Ones" (as *arrabbiato* applied to an animal in Italian means infected with rabies).

Because of the opposition and the Florentine tradition of accommodation, Savonarola's desire for a new puritanical moral order in the city largely failed, although for those who suffered under its provisions, this was not much compensation. Gambling was indeed made illegal and the brothels were shuttered; this restriction of sexual license was seen as part of the friar's policy against homosexuality. Often popularly referred to across Italy as *il vizio fiorentino*, the Florentine vice, male same-sex relations resulted, it was believed, from the late age of marriage among patrician males. The state-run brothels were designed to curb this practice by providing access to women for unmarried men and as a protection for decent women who would otherwise have been compromised by male attention outside accepted controls. There was also a humanist tradition of love between men that had deep resonance among those whose education and cultural environment had been the dialogues of Plato. Regardless of its roots, Savonarola preached for the harshest penalties for homosexuals, such as death by stoning or burning. Fortunately for the male population of the city, such terrible retribution was never pursued.

What did occur, however, was the organization of young boys, pledged by their *Piagnoni* parents, to enforce the moral purity of the city. These boys discovered places of gambling and broke up the games and dispersed the players, and, sadly, they harassed homosexuals in a pitiless manner. Allowed to parade in the city and sanctioned by Savonarola, these "Bands of Hope," with their short hair and "angelic" dress, provided evidence for the political maxim that only the most tyrannical regimes give power to children.

Women were enjoined to dress modestly, and Savonarola proposed organizing women's committees by neighborhood to enforce such restrictions. This the Signoria refused to do: giving power to boys was one thing, but giving power to adult women was far more contentious and unacceptable. So the Bands of Hope took to harassing women they thought inappropriately dressed, resulting in a degree of self-censorship among the women of the city. Ironically, many poor women had followed the friar because of his emphasis on moral reform—especially of their husbands—but patrician women were offended by the implication that they were part of a moral problem merely by being women.

Besides prostitutes (who lost their livelihood), young men (who lost their games and prostitutes), and gay men (who lost their reputations and grudging acceptance in the city), it was the Jews who suffered most under Savonarola's influence. Vigorous anti-Semitism was certainly not unique to Florence; Jewish moneylenders had been the primary source of small loans to the poor, operating more like pawnbrokers than bankers, and often demanding usurious rates of interest. The wealthy Christian banks were not interested in small loans for which wool workers' carding tools or combs might be the only collateral; there was too much work for too little profit. Hence, Jews filled the void. Savonarola was deeply anti-Semitic, calling Jews not only the slayers of Christ but also the bloodsuckers of the poor. He demanded Jews be expelled from Florence and that a state pawnbroking bank, or *Monte di Pietà*, be established. This was done at the end of 1495 and soon after the *Monte di Pietà* was in operation, and the expulsion of all Jews was passed by the Signoria. Nevertheless, the exodus of Jews did not happen because the expulsion was not enforced; those who left did so of their own accord. As a result, the expulsion order was repealed at the end of 1496.

The Burning of the Vanities

The moral terrorism of the *Piagnoni* can best to be represented by the celebrated Burning of the Vanities. Savonarola had a particular animus against the lascivious traditions of carnival in Florence. Lorenzo de'Medici himself had been the author of some songs that caused the more pious in the city to recoil from what they thought were the excesses of vice that carnival represented. Consequently, beginning with the carnival in February 1495, the traditions of license were replaced with religious processions and acts of contrition, as was appropriate for the time leading up to Lent. In that year Savonarola encouraged the faithful to bring objects that might impede religious devotion to be consigned to the flames. He was not the inventor of this practice—San Bernardino of Siena had held similar bonfires earlier in the century—but Savonarola used it to great effect. This is especially true of the February 1497 Burning of the Vanities. His Bands of Hope collected everything that might conceivably be identified as sinful by the friar, including musical instruments, cosmetics, mirrors, erotic literature (such as Catullus, Ovid, or Boccaccio), and secular art. The boys then carried these in a ritual procession to the Piazza della Signoria where they were destroyed by fire before a huge crowd.

Florentine Culture under Savonarola's Influence

Whether Sandro Botticelli, who became a fervent disciple of Savonarola, actually sacrificed some of his paintings to the Burning of the Vanities is unclear, although it is possible. His contemporary, Lorenzo di Credi, probably did, and many other images of non-religious subjects were indeed destroyed, together with rare and beautiful manuscripts.

Nevertheless, any discussion of culture under the influence of Savonarola between 1494 and 1498 must include a discussion of how some of the most committed members of that unofficial Platonic academy under Lorenzo fell under Savonarola's influence. Ficino (d. 1499) initially was a supporter of the friar but soon after backed away, living to see Savonarola's fall. Count Giovanni Pico della Mirandola, however, the author of the *Oration on the Dignity of Man*, did commit completely even before the expulsion of the Medici. He destroyed his early secular poetry and gave his fortune away to the poor. He even began the process of entering the Dominican order, only to die at thirty-one in November of 1494, just a week after Piero fled the city. Savonarola had him buried in a Dominican cowl in San Marco. There has been a lingering rumor that supporters of Piero poisoned Pico and the poet and scholar Angelo Poliziano (who died at forty in late September of 1494), but no clear evidence supports this story, although a recent examination of their remains did find traces of arsenic.

Pico's close friend and fellow member of Lorenzo's coterie was Girolamo Benivieni, a talented poet, musician, and scholar who first became interested in Platonism under Pico's influence and subsequently a *Piagnone*, led there again by Pico. It was Benivieni who translated the sermons of Savonarola into learned Latin, and he rejected his own earlier poetry, destroying some of it because it was too worldly. Thereafter, his work becomes more religious in character. Benivieni was active in the Burning of the Vanities and continued his devotion to Savonarola until the end of his long life (1453–1542), even to the point of pestering the Medici Pope Clement VII (Piero's cousin!) to posthumously lift the excommunication and charge of heresy against Savonarola.

Botticelli, another familiar of the Medici circle, and the man often identified as their painter because of works such as the *Uffizi Adoration* and *Pallas and the Centaur*, and the Neoplatonic and pagan themes so visible in *The Birth of Venus*, *Primavera*, and *The Calumny of Apelles*, did fall under the friar's influence. His work thereafter until his death in 1510 exhibited a visible devotional quality and indeed a mystical element, most evident in the *Mystic Nativity* (c. 1501), which was inspired by a sermon of Savonarola's. This change of style and his loss of commissions following the fall of Savonarola led to considerable poverty and neglect of Botticelli, an artist who once defined the visual style of Laurentian Florence.

Savonarola was himself a vernacular poet of some talent, writing religious work that is full of sincere feeling. His poetry in many ways reflects the nature of his sermons, fulminating against sin and worldliness or bathed in melancholy at the sinful nature of mankind. And, of course, his sermons, delivered in Italian and printed almost immediately, have a powerful rhetorical quality that has more to do with the medieval Dominican *ars predicandi* (the art of preaching) than Ciceronian rhetoric.

The Fall of Savonarola

The collapse of Savonarola's influence was the result of several factors working together and driven by forces both from within and without Florence. His meddling in foreign affairs, which had first raised his reputation through his negotiations with Charles VIII, now helped bring him down. First, he refused to abandon the French alliance, despite the demands of the papacy and Milan. It would have been difficult for the friar to denounce the king he had prophesied as the new Cyrus and the scourge of a corrupt Church, and whose divine mission he had blessed. Charles, however, had done nothing for him or Florence, and indeed had effectively given Pisa its independence rather than return it to Florence. The issue of Pisa was critical as a point of Florentine pride and commercial policy, and Savonarola knew it. He began to preach that God had put the fate of Pisa in his hands and that he would restore it to Florence; the Pisans thought otherwise. His failure to deliver the port city made a great many early supporters question his direct line to God.

Second, his increasingly vituperative assaults on the papacy made many Florentines afraid of the consequences of an interdict. Pope Alexander VI grew angrier at Savonarola's message of corruption in the Church, much of it directed at him personally. As early as October of 1495 Alexander sent a demand for Savonarola to cease preaching. Although he did for a while, he resumed his sermons in 1496. Alexander demanded that Savonarola travel to Rome to explain himself. The friar, however, knew that he would never leave the Holy City alive, so he claimed illness made him unfit for travel; he did send the pope a collection of sermons and prophecies, probably believing that he could influence the papacy as well. A veiled promise of a cardinal's hat if he would put his energy and skills at Alexander's service resulted in a less-than-diplomatic response from Savonarola in which the red hat was described as the color of blood. Finally in June 1497 he was excommunicated and ordered to stop preaching and saying Mass.

Savonarola again complied briefly but he resumed officiating at Mass by Christmas of that year, and in February 1498 he once more returned to his practice of incendiary Lenten sermons in the cathedral, as well as officiating at the Eucharist. The drama of the confrontation between the pope and the friar resulted in larger-than-ever crowds of common people attending the sermons, but engendered strong reservations among the mercantile classes who feared papal retaliation through an interdict and interference with foreign trade and banking.

Internally, the position of the *Piagnoni* was becoming insecure as well. The model of the Bands of Hope gave rise to gangs of anti-Savonarolan youths, known as *compagnacci*. These were a combination of violent street boys and some young patricians angered by the suppression of their traditional pleasures and activities. The calm and virtuous order imposed by Savonarola and his supporters had begun to break down, with threats and scenes of violence and intimidation visible from both factions, including *compagnacci* infiltrating and disturbing sermons by Savonarola and his disciples. Moreover, the attempt at reconciliation with former Medici supporters, a policy Savonarola counseled from the moment Piero was expelled, unraveled as a consequence of growing elite nostalgia for the old regime, the insecurity in the city, the dangers posed by the papacy, and a more active Medici faction working to restore Piero to bring stability to Florence.

In April of 1497 Piero himself with a small force had appeared outside the city. Nothing came of this seemingly quixotic attempt to reestablish the Medici in the city, but later it was discovered that there had been a much more serious conspiracy associated with this event, one from within Florence, orchestrated by prominent patricians. The identification of the patrician ringleaders led to a trial in which they were all condemned to death. Savonarola had previously counseled mercy for both active and former *Palleschi*, and the law permitted these men to appeal directly to the new Great Council. Nevertheless, after a speech by the most vocal and fervent of the *Piagnoni*, Francesco Valori, the right of appeal was waived and the men executed. It is hard to believe that Savonarola did not encourage Valori in his advice not to permit an appeal, despite the law and his earlier policy of reconciliation.

Indeed, Savonarola was becoming more aggressive in his rejection of the pope's demand that he not perform sacerdotal functions or preach in the city. He said Mass during the Christmas celebrations of 1497, and his preaching resumed in the Cathedral during Lent of 1498, both in direct contravention of Alexander VI's orders. On discovering the Dominican's contumacious disregard of a papal injunction, the pope voiced what so many members of the mercantile elite of the city feared: unless Savon-arola was silenced, the city would be put under an interdict and the trade, property, and business prospects of Florentines abroad would be com-promised. Although he still enjoyed considerable support, Savonarola was told to cease his public preaching by the Signoria. He obeyed but returned to his base at San Marco where he continued to meet with and encourage his supporters.

Savonarola's Arrest, Trial, and Execution

At last the Signoria had shown that it was willing to confront Savonarola and the *Piagnoni*. This motivated the enemies of Savonarola and the *Arra-bbiati* in the city to action. The initial response came from the Franciscan Order. These friars minor had seen attendance at their sermons decline and donations collapse. Moreover, in some ways, Savonarola had also sto-len many of the Franciscan's traditions in his prophecies. For example, it was once believed that the Joachimite prophecies would be fulfilled by the Franciscans, and here was a Dominican claiming that tradition for his order. The preachers to the poor and marginalized were usually Fran-ciscans (especially the banned *Fraticelli*), whereas the Dominicans were inquisitors and teachers, but now Savonarola claimed to speak for the poor and women. Consequently, in this competition for souls and sanc-tity, the Franciscans played a truly spiritual card: Savonarola was chal-lenged to an Ordeal by Fire! It is only in this environment of prophecy, spiritual competition, and essential matters of faith that such a test could even be contemplated; this was, after all, still the city of hardheaded mer-chants and Platonic philosophers.

Savonarola had no choice but to accept the match. He and a Franciscan were to walk across burning coals and the one who emerged unscathed would be God's chosen. The ordeal was set for April 7 in the Piazza della Signoria. When Savonarola and his two seconds arrived, there was instantly an argument over costume, precedence, and other issues that kept the huge crowd of assembled citizens waiting. Then a dramatic rain-storm extinguished the flames and the angry and now skeptical crowd dispersed. Savonarola's command of his credulous followers was shaken, giving his now more numerous and powerful enemies opportunity to silence him altogether.

Figure 12. Filippo Dolciati (1443–1519), The Burning of Savonarola
and Two Disciples (Silvestro Maruffi and Domenico Buonvicini)
on May 23, 1498. (Image via Wikimedia, public domain.)

Questions were openly raised: If Savonarola had been God's instrument on earth, why could he not, as he continually claimed to be able to do, return Pisa to Florence? Why was the extremely expensive and unsuccessful war to reclaim the seaport needed if it was in the Dominican's gift? Why was the weather in the winter of 1497–1498 so wet and terrible, resulting in failed crops and such high prices for bread that there was much suffering in the city among the poor? What if Alexander made good on his threats and put the city under an interdict? What benefit was there now in clinging to the French alliance, particularly given the cavalier attitude of Charles VIII to Florence's exposed position and the prophetic news that he died at just twenty-eight on April 7, 1498, the very day of the Ordeal by Fire?

On April 8 (Palm Sunday) a furious crowd laid siege to San Marco while a band of violent *compagnacci* thugs killed the patrician *Piagnone* spokesman, Francesco Valori, together with his wife, in his palace in retribution for the speech denying an appeal to the five aristocratic conspirators. Other *Piagnoni* leaders were threatened, but once the hated Valori was dead the anger was again focused on San Marco. Savonarola was apprehended with his two closest disciples and taken to the Palazzo della Signoria where they were examined under torture. Savonarola admitted that his prophecies did not come from God and that he, as a priest and a foreigner, had no right to engage in political activity in Florence. He was then reexamined by officials sent from the pope: they declared him to be a heretic and surrendered him to the secular arm for punishment, which would be death. Girolamo Savonarola was taken with his two closest followers to the Piazza where they were hanged, their bodies burned, and the ashes thrown into the Arno to ensure that no relics would be collected to inspire the remaining *Piagnoni*. With his death the experiment of the New Jerusalem ended.

AFTERWORD

The death of Savonarola did not end the divisions in the city. The Great Council continued to witness the struggle between the supporters of popular government and those patricians who wished a return to some form of oligarchy (*governo stretto*). The economic situation did not much improve either because of the cost of the war with Pisa and the need to establish some measure of security for the city and the *contado* in a very unstable age. The new king of France, Louis XII, was determined to follow the example of Charles VIII and invade Italy, this time with Milan his primary goal. Before the premature death of his cousin, he had been the duke of Orleans, and his grandmother had been a daughter of Giangaleazzo Visconti. It was obvious that Italy would once more become the battlefield of Europe.

Furthermore, the Medici continued to inject an element of instability—or hope, depending on your factional complexion. Piero had conveniently died at the end of December 1503, drowned while retreating with the French army after the Battle of Garigliano. His death removed the most objectionable of the Medici pretenders to Florentine rule, so there was some expectation that the divisions in the city might be healed by their return. However, the head of the family was now Cardinal Giovanni de'Medici, whose ambitions were in Rome. Nevertheless, a vital Medici faction continued to operate in the city, one that would ultimately prove victorious in 1512.

The Great Council outlived Savonarola and continued to function, although riven by the same divisions that characterized the city, particularly between the wealthy patricians of ancient descent and those *novi cives*, the new men of mercantile wealth but little lineage. The instability of the situation at the turn of the sixteenth century resulted in Piero Soderini being named *gonfaloniere* for life in 1502. Niccolo Machiavelli was his second chancellor. There was hope that this arrangement would give some measure of continuity to government, and Soderini was a good compromise, as his brother had been one of the leaders of the *Piagnoni* party and devoted to Savonarola, while another brother was a cardinal who was close to Giovanni de'Medici. Despite some Florentine successes, such as finally recapturing Pisa in 1506, the position of independent republics was precarious in Italy, divided as it was between the ambitions of the Spanish and the French.

Like his predecessors in office, Soderini clung to the French alliance; however, the tide was turning in favor of the Spaniards. Pope Julius II created the Holy League to drive the French from the peninsula, and Cardinal Giovanni de' Medici became one of Julius' trusted advisers and legate. Julius acceded to Giovanni's request to restore the Medici to Florence by means of a Spanish army. The republic attempted to resist the professional, battle-hardened troops of the Holy League through the defense of Prato by the citizen militia that Machiavelli had trained and equipped. The result was a complete rout of the Florentines and the flight of Piero Soderini. Then, on September 1, 1512, Giuliano de' Medici, the youngest son of Lorenzo the Magnificent, re-entered the city, followed on September 4 by Cardinal Giovanni in great state. The Great Council was dissolved and the Medici reclaimed possession of the palace on the Via Larga that Cosimo had built. Soon after, the institutions of the republic that had emerged after the 1494 expulsion were dismantled and the Medici reassumed rule of the city. Although they were to be expelled one more time, following the Sack of Rome in 1527 in the time of another Medici pope, Clement VII (the illegitimate son of Lorenzo's brother, Giuliano, murdered in the Pazzi Conspiracy), they were returned again with a Spanish army in 1530. This time the Medici would remain in power first as dukes of Florence, then grand dukes of Etruria and grand dukes of Tuscany until the extinction of the family in 1737, after having produced two queens of France (Catherine de' Medici, consort of Henri II, and Marie de' Medici, consort of Henri IV).

The history of Florence, then, is very much the story of the Medici family, at least after 1434. They were first political bosses, manipulators of the republican commune in a way that provided stability and continuity for a government where neither was easily achieved because of the nature of the constitution and the ambitions of the powerful families in the city. Lorenzo became something like an uncrowned prince, especially after 1480, but one whose personal qualities and style helped define an age and bring luster to the city. The failure of this system was evident in the short and disastrous regime of Piero di Lorenzo, whose expulsion in 1494 at a very perilous moment in Italian history led to the ascendancy of Girolamo Savonarola, who managed through his prophecies and Christian ambitions for Florence to fill the power vacuum created by the exile of the family that had led the city for sixty years. But he, too, fell as a consequence of his and his followers' hubris, his clumsy foreign policy, factional division, and his inability to deliver what he had promised. His short period of ascendency, November 1494–April 1498, was in some ways a curious anomaly in the narrative of Florence in the Renaissance, but it also reflected a great many of the currents of thought and belief that always rested just below the surface of the Laurentian regime. The New Rome briefly was transformed into the New Jerusalem, but ultimately returned not as a revitalized Roman Republic but as a monarchical new Roman Empire under Medici rule in 1530, and Jerusalem fell to the Turks.

The Significance of the Age of the Medici and Savonarola

All historical moments have an ability to provide insights into why the world is the way it is: we are all the products of those who went before us, lived their lives solving the problems of their age, and sought what they thought best for their immediate societies or the wider context of the human family. Today we would not all agree with any of these solutions and would find some extremely distasteful, but that does not make our need to understand these decisions and the circumstances that give rise to them any less important. In studying the past we study ourselves from a more distant perspective and that itself is of the greatest significance.

When the sixty-four years of Florentine history between 1434 and 1498 are investigated, some general themes emerge which add to our knowledge of why societies respond in the ways that they do, and how certain fundamental problems repeat themselves or seem impossible to resolve. This analysis of the Florence of the Medici and Savonarola illustrates, for example, how the question of where political power should reside caused such friction in the Florentine republic that was never successfully solved. Was the republic a government for and by all mature citizens the best regime for the city (*governo largo*) or should more power be given to those who had the greatest stake in society, those with wealth, experience, and property (*governo stretto*)? All societies face this dilemma to some degree, but the issue was particularly corrosive in Florence. The 1293 Ordinances of Justice and the years that followed defined who would have access to elected office and the conditions that had to be met to enter political life: guild membership, maturity for resident adult males, not being in arrears of taxes, and not too closely related to those in positions of significant authority. These were extremely liberal and reasonable, especially for an Italian commune in the late thirteenth century.

What emerged, however, was not a reasonable, smoothly functioning government that lasted for centuries, but an unstable and uncertain republic that on several occasions sought the intervention of "men on horseback" to solve these problems and then, ideally, withdraw. The instability came from sources that no set of laws can ever address: personal and clan ambition, personal alliances or enmity, divergent economic interests, conflicting ties of family and public interest, just to note the most obvious. Consequently, Florentines saw each other with great distrust, and this in itself often exacerbated the very problems listed above. Because the executive of the republic was a committee of nine men who held office for only two months, it was difficult to pursue a coherent and consistent policy; because faction was often more important than the public good, the commune suffered.

So does this mean that the victory of the Medici faction following the return of Cosimo in 1434 was inevitable? Was the republic ungovernable without a strong hand to guide it? In its history nothing was ever inevitable, but certain things happened for certain reasons, and these led to particular consequences. The success of Cosimo and his regime was his controlling—not extinguishing—factional, class, and personal competition during his lifetime. He wisely left the republican constitution in place and managed it carefully from behind the scenes, taking care not to offend the pride and sensitivities of the powerful patrician clans while equally not ignoring the less privileged, as the Albizzi Oligarchy eventually did. Cosimo also saw the value of using his spectacular wealth to make his city more famous and beautiful, a policy that endeared him to the population, regardless of their condition. He recognized that Florence—and Italy—needed peace, so he worked closely with Milan, once Florence's most feared enemy, and subscribed to the Peace of Lodi and the Italian League (1454 and 1455). The regime he constructed in the thirty years he managed the Florentine state achieved a level of stability, and cultural and diplomatic, as well as economic, success that he earned the honor of the city as *Pater Patriae*.

Later historians have debated whether Cosimo destroyed a vital, functioning republic or whether he brought a level of stability, peace, and coherence to a city so riven by faction, class, and insecurity that some form of management was inevitable, and the Medici introduced the most benign form of control possible. There is no doubt but that some voices were silenced and some individuals suffered; consequently, the question really to be answered by all students of this period is whether the sacrifices were worth it.

If we look to the city itself, Florentines in 1464 obviously thought that the Medici regime was still the best option because on Cosimo's death his son Piero assumed his authority without serious opposition. Later, however, when Piero showed himself unable to manage the republic in the same astute manner as Cosimo, opposition to Medici rule became vocal and perilous to both the family and the faction. It was not all Piero's fault: he was in pain, ill, and not able to follow his father's example. And, from the instant of Cosimo's death, powerful men and families saw the end of Medici dominance and an opportunity to reassert their traditional influence over the republic. Thus, the growing hostility to the Medici revealed that true republican principles remained just below the surface and would emerge as the Medici faltered. Again, the historiographical question arises: To what extent does the personality and ability of the ruler drive the ability of the state to succeed? Had Piero lived longer, it is not impossible to imagine him being removed from office and the Medici faction exiled, as had happened to the Albizzi oligarchs and other groups in power. We can say this because in the late 1460s there was still an alternative waiting in the wings in the form of a return to the pristine republic, no longer managed by the Medici. It was a viable option and one easily installed, should it be required.

Piero's early death in 1469 made the need to activate this still-vital republican ideology unnecessary. His son, Lorenzo di Piero, the Magnificent, was accepted as the leader of the Medici machine immediately, despite his youth. His personality and his great abilities and skill in managing people and situations provided another reason to again embrace the Medici hegemony. The events of the Pazzi Conspiracy and the war that resulted from it indicated in a very bloody way that there was still opposition to the Medici among some great patrician clans. But Lorenzo's masterful personal diplomacy and his good luck allowed him to escape the very real dangers and return to Florence as a hero. Had there been widespread, significant hostility to the Medici in Florence it would have been easy to evict their faction and leave Lorenzo to the anger of Pope Sixtus IV. It did not happen.

The events of 1478–1480, however, did change the nature of the regime. Lorenzo's brother had been murdered and he very nearly had been as well; Florence had been attacked and her territories ravaged. Lorenzo, then, created the Council of Seventy for tighter political control and started altogether behaving much more like a prince. It was this change in Medici management techniques that really turned Florence from a republic, where republican principles lay in reserve should regime change be required, to a quasi-monarchy, with Lorenzo as an uncrowned prince. As such he used the great patricians and political classes less and his personal household more; he took public money for private use and separated himself out from the dominant culture of Florence by creating a courtly world of Neoplatonic thought, complex classical allusions, arcane references, and recondite images. This Laurentian culture was one of the glories of the Italian Renaissance, but it also removed the Medici from the popular base it once enjoyed. So, again, the historiographical question arises whether the Medici could sustain its power, given the traditions of the republic, when its leader seemed no longer part of the dominant culture of the vast majority of the citizens he ruled.

Lorenzo's personal gifts and ability to sustain some measure of stable, effective government—and the memory of his stunning victory over his enemies—caused little overt opposition to his rule until near the end of his life. Then his illness and the dangerous situation in Italy and abroad, as well as the growing popularity of the Dominican prior of San Marco, Girolamo Savonarola, began to erode his authority. His tragically early death allowed his son, Piero di Lorenzo, to take power in the name of his family. But from the outset it was clear that Piero was not up to the challenges of his times. When he capitulated to the French king, Charles VIII, in 1494, he proved how far his talents were from those of his father. He was expelled and the Medici faction dissolved. Again, it is important to ask whether a regime like the Medici hegemony was capable of longterm power because it was neither a republic nor a monarchy: it was a curious combination of both, but one so dependent on the abilities of its leader that eventually the disjunction between necessity and competence would result in its collapse. This is what happened in the case of Piero, and it is a cautionary example for other hybrid political structures.

Moreover, by 1494 the republican traditions so very much alive, if dormant, in the 1460s had become vestigial at best. And the old question of whether the government should be exclusive or inclusive (*governo stretto* or *largo*) had still not been resolved. There was, then, in 1494 a power vacuum, as the Medici had succeeded in silencing their enemies and drawing many citizens of all classes into their orbit. The vacuum was filled, not by a faction of oligarchs or by a popular government, or even a renewed Ciompi revolt, but by a Dominican monk, Savonarola, whose authority came from not being part of any group and whose power, he claimed, superseded any faction or clan because it came directly from God. To what extent, then, was Savonarola another of those "men on horseback"—actually in his case it would have been a mule—like Charles of Calabria or Walter of Brienne? He was not a citizen and was a priest, hence outside every category of traditional political influence. But he enjoyed moral authority, he had the good fortune to have made some lucky prophecies, and he connected huge numbers of the population with their deepest traditions and beliefs, ones largely ignored by Lorenzo. He spoke of God's plan and called for asceticism and sacrifice, for Christian values and the practice of piety. He reminded those traditionally pious citizens who listened to his sermons of the Italian medieval prophetic tradition, the exaltation of the poor by the *Fraticelli*, and of Florentine exceptionalism, even as propounded by the humanist Leonardo Bruni. His message, then, was in reality very mainstream but delivered by a voice from outside the old centers of power.

The harsh moral order Savonarola imposed, not to speak of his disastrous foreign policy and other failures, alienated a great many Florentines, who once more began to form opposition factions or even call for the return of the Medici. But Savonarola did deliver a new constitution that reflected the widest form of wide government. The Great Council was a Florentine experiment in a form of popular sovereignty, even if Savonarola claimed that sovereignty really came directly from God. This council was an attempt to address the problems we have identified as inherent in the Florentine system by deciding finally that the widest expression of political opinion should be heard and that the high offices of the state should take their authority from the Great Council. Of course the old patrician clans, hoping for a return to some form of oligarchy, were opposed, but many were seduced by the idea of a Florence without the Medici, governed instead by its people.

It would not last. The failures of Savonarola and his *Piagnoni* party, together with the hostility of the papacy and powerful groups in the city, brought down the Dominican after just over three and a half years. What is instructive, however, is that after the trial and execution of Savonarola his Great Council continued, although after 1502 with Piero Soderini as *gonfaloniere* for life, a popular replacement for the Medici. Florence had learned that it needed a stable, coherent regime to manage the republic.

With the Medici and Savonarola gone, it fell to the leader of a faction, at least a Florentine. Even this new attempt at stability was not to last: in 1512 the Medici were returned with the help of a Spanish army supported by the papacy. It seemed as though Florence and the Medici had become too mutually dependent to be separated for long, a circumstance rehearsed in 1530, after the 1527 expulsion.

This book, then, is an investigation of how states experiment in granting power to individuals, factions, and groups, and how ambitious individuals and groups grasp power at moments of crisis. It is a very important story to tell both because of the cultural importance of Florence in the fifteenth century and because of the evidence it provides of the extreme difficulty in solving political problems built into a community's history and structure. In time, the Medici abandoned any attempt to accommodate that culture of republicanism and the exalted pride of the patrician families. Following their last expulsion, the Medici returned as princes in both authority and name. The republican institutions, memories, and traditions were consciously and often violently suppressed so all that remained was the absolute power of the prince, a Medici, Cosimo I, who would eventually become Grand Duke of Tuscany and whose dynasty would rule unopposed for two centuries.

DOCUMENTS

DOCUMENT 1

Guelfs and Ghibellines, 1347[1]

Florence established itself as a Guelf (pro-papal) commune, privileging the members of this faction to the exclusion of the pro-imperial Ghibellines. This legislation excluded Ghibellines who had opposed the Guelfs from holding office, and encouraged Guelfs to identify Ghibellines to deny them positions of authority in the commune.

The lord priors have heard and comprehended the expositions and supplications made to them . . . by zealous Guelfs who are loyal to the Holy Roman Church, to the effect that the Guelfs of the city, *contado*, and district of Florence . . . have always striven for the glory and honor of Mother Church and they intend to continue to do so with all of their power. [They assert that] there are some who are not only rebels of Mother Church, but also of the *popolo* and Commune of Florence, who have insinuated themselves into the administration and government of the city of Florence and with iniquitous and deceitful word and operations, endeavor to separate devoted and faithful children from their venerated mother. . . . So the abovementioned lord priors desire to have the Holy Roman Church as the mother of her Guelf children, and to prevent those seeking to sow discord from achieving their goals and from interfering in the administration of the Florentine republic, which is to be ruled and governed by true Guelfs. . . . In honor, praise, and reverence of the omnipotent God and the glorious Virgin, and in exaltation and augmentation

---

1. From Gene Brucker, ed. and trans., *The Society of Renaissance Florence: A Documentary Study* (New York: Harper Torchbooks, 1971), doc. 41.

of Mother Church and the magnificent Parte Guelfa . . . they provide, ordain and decree the following:

First, no Ghibelline who has been condemned and outlawed for rebellion since November 1, 1300 . . . or who has rebelled (or will rebel in the future) . . . against the *popolo* and Commune of Florence . . . or his son or descendant . . . in the male line . . . may hold any office of the *popolo* and Commune of Florence or any office in the Parte Guelfa or . . . in any guild. . . .

If any doubt should arise concerning any person or persons who are drawn for, or elected to any of the abovementioned offices, that he might be or is said to be one of those prohibited, then there should be held . . . a deliberation of the lord priors . . . [with their colleges] . . . whether or not that person should be removed from office. And if it is decided by a majority of them by secret vote . . . then he is to be removed from that office. . . .

Anyone may accuse [or] denounce [a person] and notify [the authorities] about the abovementioned cases . . . and the podestà, captain, and executor . . . must take cognizance of this and proceed by means of an inquisition, and punish and condemn [the guilty]. . . . And for proof, the testimony of six reputable witnesses suffices. . . .

DOCUMENT 2

Best Practices for Florentine Merchants in the Fourteenth Century[2]

Paolo da Certaldo (c. 1320–c. 1370), the son of a success-ful notary, was a grain merchant, as well as writer and friend of Giovanni Boccaccio. His Libro dei buoni costumi *(Book of Good Practices) is an insight into the values, mentality, and character of the Florentine mercantile elite in the mid-fourteenth century.*

251. If you are a merchant, and letters for you arrive along with other letters, always remember to read your own letters first before giving the other letters to the people to whom they are addressed. And if your let-ters should advise you to buy or sell some merchandise for your own advantage, call immediately for your agent, and do what the letters say, and then hand over the other letters that came with yours. But don't give them until you have concluded your transactions, because those other letters might say things that could ruin your own dealings, and the service that you would have done to your friend or neighbour or some stranger would turn into great evil. You are not obliged to help others if it is a dis-service to your own affairs.

252. When your sons are small, place them in the trade in which you want them to become masters, for whatever they learn and practise as children, they will retain and love as adults. Likewise I tell you to send them to be raised and trained in a profession or trade in whatever coun-try, town, or city where you wish them to be citizens or inhabitants. And do not say: "I will send him as a boy to France, and there he shall grow up and be raised, and learn the ways of merchants in France, so that when he is thirty years old or so, he can return to Florence." In this way, he will not

---

2. From *The Book of Good Practices* of Paolo da Certaldo, in Vittore Branca, *Merchant Writers: Florentine Memoirs from the Middle Ages and Renaissance*, trans. Murtha Baca (Toronto: University of Toronto Press, 2015), 66.

be as good a merchant in Florence as he was in France, for he has been raised and has grown up and has made many friends there, and his heart will always be in France. And at every difficulty he has in Florence, he will say: "If I were in France, I wouldn't be going through this!" And the same goes for other countries.

DOCUMENT 3

Excerpts from the *Ordinances of Justice*, 1293[3]

This legislation constituted the legal framework of the guild republic following the victory of the Guelf guildsmen over the magnates and grandi *in 1293. The twenty-one guilds recognized by the commune were named and the responsibilities of their members noted. Also, the authority of the commune to prosecute magnates and ensure their obedience to the law was clearly stated.*

[I] Concerning the fellowship, union, promise, and oath of the Guilds expressed in the Ordinance contained below:

Since that most perfect [ordinance] was approved, which is valid in all its parts and approved by the judgement of all; therefore, by the aforesaid lords Podestà, Defender and Captain, Priors of the Guilds, and learned men, by the authority of the aforesaid *balìa*, it is ordained and provided that the twelve greater Guilds, namely:

The Guild of Judges and Notaries
The Guild of Calimala Merchants [cloth traders and finishers]
The Guild of Money Changers
The Guild of Wool Merchants
The Guild of the Merchants of Por Santa Maria [the silk guild]
The Guild of Physicians and Apothecaries
The Guild of Furriers
The Guild of Butchers
The Guild of Shoemakers
The Guild of Blacksmiths
The Guild of Master Stoneworkers and Carpenters
The Guild of Used Clothing Sellers

---

3. From Gaetano Salvemini, *Magnati e popolani in Firenze dal 1280 al 1295* (Firenze: Carnescchi e figli, 1899), 385–86, 394–95. Translation by Kirsty Schut.

and also all the other Guilds of the city of Florence that are written below, which are these, namely:

The Guild of Wine Sellers
The Guild of Greater Innkeepers
The Guild of Sellers of Salt and Oil and Cheese
The Guild of Greater Leatherworkers
The Guild of Armorers and Sword Makers
The Guild of Locksmiths and Old and New Iron Workers
The Guild of Saddlers and Shield-makers
The Guild of Greater Carpenters
The Guild of Bakers

which have flags and are accustomed to have flags from the Commune of Florence for five years hence, and the craftsmen of these Guilds, by the protection of which and of whom it is assured that the city and Commune of Florence is defended, ought to and are required to legitimately appoint suitable Syndics who are sufficiently trained with regards to each and every thing written below, within the time that shall be fixed for the Rectors or Consuls of each of the said Guilds by the lords Defender and Captain (which they are required to do in the present month of January that we are in), namely that each of these Guilds [should appoint] one from their own Guild. These Syndics, with a full and sufficient mandate, should and ought to appear before the lord Captain and Defender of the city of Florence with their followers remaining in the power of that lord Defender and Captain. And the same Syndics should swear, physically touching the Bible, exactly what the aforesaid lord Captain shall wish to compose as an oath of allegiance for them. And the aforesaid Syndics should also promise each other to take care that the Guilds of which they are and will be Syndics, and the men of the same Guilds, will hold and observe a good and pure and faithful fellowship and company with the other Guilds, and the men of those Guilds. And [they should promise] that they will be unanimous and in agreement together concerning the honour and defense and exaltation and the peaceful and tranquil state of the lords Podestà, Captain and Defender, and the offices of the lords Priors and the standard bearer of justice and the Guilds and artisans of the city and commune of Florence and the entire population of Florence. [. . .]

[VI] Concerning the penalties imposed and ordained against the Magnati *[Magnates] who offend against the* Popolani *[common citizens]*

It is also ordained and provided that if any of the *Magnati* of the city or district of Florence in any way, namely zealously or with premeditation, kill or have killed, or wound or have wounded any of the *Popolani* of the city or district of Florence in such a way that death follows from those wounds or that wound, the lord Podestà should impose a capital sentence on such a *Magnatus* who does such a wicked deed or has it done, and each one of them, namely those who did the deed as well as those who had it done, so that his head and each of their heads will be cut off so that he dies, if he should come into the power of the Commune of Florence. And likewise the Podestà ought and is required to have all of his and their goods devastated and destroyed, and when they have been destroyed and devastated they should be confiscated by the Commune of Florence and he should make them come to the Commune of Florence. If such malefactors do not come into the power of the Commune of Florence, they will nonetheless be assigned the death penalty, in such a way that if at any time they do come into the power of the Commune of Florence, his head or their heads will be cut off so that they die, and all of their goods will be devastated and destroyed, and when they have been devastated they will come to the Commune of Florence. And likewise the guarantors of such *Magnati* and malefactors, who provided surety for the same malefactors to the Commune of Florence, should and ought to be compelled by the lord Podestà to pay to the Commune of Florence that quantity of money for which they gave surety for that *Magnatus* and malefactor, or another one of them. And a careful estimation of the value of such goods should be made in order that such a guarantor may have recompense for that quantity of money from the goods of such a malefactor that have been devastated and destroyed. And whatever is left over from those goods should come to the Commune of Florence.

DOCUMENT 4

The Arrival of Walter of Brienne from Giovanni Villani's *New Chronicle*[4]

Giovanni Villani (c. 1276/1280—1348) was a Florentine merchant, a member of the Guild of Wool Finishers, who held high office in the city as a prior and as a diplomat. In 1300 he began his Chronicle (La Nuova Cronica or New Chronicle) recording significant events in the history of the city. He included statistics, observations, and information that would otherwise not have been known, making his Chronicle an important source for the fourteenth century. Villani died of the plague in 1348, but his Chronicle was continued by his brother and then his nephew.

Here begins the thirteenth book, which tells how the Duke of Athens took over the lordship of Florence, and what followed.

Now we must begin the thirteenth book, because the style of our treatise requires it and because it contains new material: both great changes and unusual revolutions occurred in these days in our city of Florence because of our conflicts between citizens and because of the bad government of the Twenty. These things were so unusual that I, the author, who was present, doubt that they will be believed by our successors, and yet they happened in just the way we shall recount. The noble, great, and ill-fated host had returned from Lucca and that city had been surrendered to the Pisans and the Florentines saw that they were in a bad state. They saw that their captain, Messer Malatesta, had not handled himself well in the war and were fearful of his treaty with the Bavarian, which we touched on earlier. At the beginning of June 1342, [with an eye to] making themselves more secure, they elected the Frenchman Messer Walter, duke of Athens and count of Brienne as captain and conservator of the *popolo* for the same salary and with the same knights and foot soldiers that Messer Malatesta had had, for the period of one year. And for his pleasure, or out of shrewdness—for this soon became evident—he

---

4. From Giovanni Villani on the arrival of Walter of Brienne, in *The Final Book of Giovanni Villani's New Chronicle*, trans. Matthew Thomas Sneider (Kalamazoo, MI: Medieval Institute Publications, Western Michigan University, 2016), 25–26.

wished to return with his people to Santa Croce, to the house of the Friars Minor. Once Messer Malatesta's term was over in August, the Duke of Athens was also made captain general and given the right to administer justice inside and outside the city. This gentleman, seeing the city divided and being greedy for money, which he needed because he was a wayfarer and pilgrim—although he held title to the duchy of Athens, he did not possess it—was seduced by certain *grandi*, who were constantly seeking to destroy the ordinances of the *popolo*, and by certain rich *popolani*, who wished to be lords of the city and avoid repaying their debts to their creditors (this because their companies were in a bad state, a matter which we will need to recount at a later time and in another place). These people went continually to Santa Croce, by day and night, advising him to take the lordship of the city entirely into his own hands. The duke, for the reasons stated above, and longing for lordship, began to follow this wicked advice. He became cruel and tyrannical, with the excuse that he was doing justice—as we will show in the next chapter—in order to make himself feared, and make himself wholly Lord of Florence.

DOCUMENT 5

A Merchant's Conscience from the *Ricordanze* (Memoir) of Gregorio Dati[5]

Gregorio di Stagio Dati (1362–1435) was a silk merchant and hence a member of the Guild of Por Santa Maria. He held numerous guild and communal offices in Florence, including standard bearer of justice. His diary (ricordanze) *is an important source of social and economic insight into his times and his* History of Florence *from 1380–1405 a record of the struggle between Florence and Milan.*

May 3rd of the year of our Lord 1412. On 28 April my name was drawn as Standard-bearer of my Company. Until that time, I had not been sure whether my name was in the rolls of the College, and yet I desired it both for my own honour and that of those who shall remain after me. I remember that Stagio, my father, held many offices in his lifetime, and was several times a magistrate of the Guild of Porta Santa Maria, and of the Merchants' Council of Five, and a tax official and a chamberlain; but his name was never drawn for any of the Colleges in his life, though shortly after his death his name was drawn as a Prior. And I remember that eight years ago I underwent many adversities on account of my business in Catalonia, and that last year I had to take care not to be arrested for debt to the City of Florence. On the very day that I was chosen for this office, a quarter of an hour before, I had finished paying my debt to the city thanks to a reprieve, which was an inspiration from God, may he always be praised and blessed. Now that I can secure other offices, it seems to me that I have received a great blessing, and I should be content with being able to say that I have sat once in the Colleges and should aspire no further. So, lest I be ungrateful or become too hungry for power (for the more men have, the more they want), I have decided and resolved that henceforth I shall never ask anyone to help me obtain whatever public offices there might be up for selection or voting, but rather I

5. Excerpt from *The Secret Book of Goro Dati*, in Vittore Branca, *Merchant Writers*, 371–72.

shall let those who are in charge of such things do their job, and abide by God's will. I shall accept whatever public or guild office for which I might be chosen, not refusing the work but obeying the call, and I shall do whatever good I can. In this way I shall avoid the vice of ambition and presumptuousness, and shall live in freedom without having to demean myself by begging for favours. And if I should depart from this resolve, each time I do so I condemn myself to give two gold florins in alms within a month. I have made this resolution in my fiftieth year.

This same day, for the good and security of my conscience, knowing myself to be weak in the face of sin, I resolve never to accept any office, should my name be drawn, in which I would have the power to exercise the death penalty. And if I should depart from this resolution, I condemn myself to give twenty-five gold florins to the poor within three months of accepting such an office. And I shall in no wise attempt to influence those who make the selections for such offices, either by asking them to put forth or not to put forth my name, but shall let them do as they see fit. And every time I might fail to do so, I condemn myself to donate a gold florin.

DOCUMENT 6

The Demands of the Ciompi, 1378[6]

The uprising of the disenfranchised poorer citizens (popolo minuto) in 1378 resulted in the temporary creation of three new guilds to represent them, giving them access to public office. A wool-carder, Michele di Lando, was thrust into a position of leadership of the popolo minuto and emerged as a spokesman for the insurgents. The demands of the Ciompi addressed the issues they identified as the causes of their oppression.

Excerpt from the Cronache e memorie del tumulto dei Ciompi.

[July 21, 1378] When the *popolo* and the guildsmen had seized the palace [of the podestà], they sent a message to the Signoria . . . that they wished to make certain demands by means of petitions, which were just and reasonable. . . . They said that, for the peace and repose of the city, they wanted certain things which they had decided among themselves . . . and they begged the priors to have them read, and then to deliberate on them, and to present them to their colleges. . . .

The first chapter [of the petition] stated that the Lana guild would no longer have a [police] official of the guild. Another was that the combers, carders, trimmers, washers, and other cloth workers would have their own [guild] consuls, and would no longer be subject to the Lana guild. Another chapter [stated that] the Commune's funded debt would no longer pay interest, but the capital would be restored [to the shareholders] within twelve years. . . . Another chapter was that all outlaws and those who had been condemned by the Commune . . . except rebels and traitors would be pardoned. Moreover, all penalties involving a loss of a limb would be cancelled, and those who were condemned would pay a money fine. . . . Furthermore, for two years none of the poor people could be prosecuted for debts of 50 florins or less. For a period of six months, no forced loans were to be levied. . . . And within that six months' period, a schedule for levying direct taxes [*estimo*] was to be compiled. . . .

---

6. From Brucker, *The Society of Renaissance Florence: A Documentary Study*, doc. 116, 236–69.

The popolo entered the palace and [the podestà] departed, without any harm being done to him. They ascended the bell tower and placed there the emblem of the blacksmiths' guild, that is, the tongs. Then the banners of the other guilds, both great and small, were unfurled from the windows of the [palace of the] podestà, and also the standard of justice, but there was no flag of the Lana guild. Those inside the palace threw out and burned . . . every document which they found. And they remained there, all that day and night, in honor of God. Both rich and poor were there, each one to protect the standard of his guild.

The next morning the *popolo* brought the standard of justice from the palace and they marched, all armed, to the Piazza della Signoria, shouting: "Long live the *popolo minuto!*" . . . Then they began to cry "that the Signoria should leave, and if they didn't wish to depart, they would be taken to their homes." Into the piazza came a certain Michele di Lando, a wool-comber, who was the son of Monna Simona, who sold provisions to the prisoners in the Stinche . . . and he was seized and the standard of justice placed in his hands. . . . Then the *popolo* ordered the priors to abandon the palace. It was well furnished with supplies necessary [for defense] but they were frightened men and they left [the palace], which was the best course. Then the *popolo* entered, taking with them the standard of justice . . . and they entered all the rooms and they found many ropes which [the authorities] had bought to hang the poor people. . . . Several young men climbed the bell tower and rang the bells to signal the victory which they had won in seizing the palace, in God's honor. Then they decided to do everything necessary to fortify themselves and to liberate the *popolo minuto*. Then they acclaimed the wool-comber, Michele di Lando, as *signore* and standard bearer of justice, and he was *signore* for two days. . . . Then [the *popolo*] decided to call other priors who would be good comrades and who would fill up the office of those priors who had been expelled. And so by acclamation, they named eight priors and the Twelve and the [Sixteen] standard-bearers.

When they wished to convene a council, these priors called together the colleges and the consuls of the guilds. . . . This council enacted a decree that everyone who had been proscribed as a Ghibelline since 1357 was to be restored to Guelf status. . . . And this was done to give a part to more people, and so that each would be content, and each would have a share of the offices, and so that all of the citizens would be united. Thus poor men would have their due, for they have always borne the expenses [of government], and only the rich have profited.

... And when they deliberated to expand the lower guilds, and where there had been fourteen, there would now be seventeen, and thus they would be stronger, and this was done. The first new guild comprised those who worked in the woolen industry: factors, brokers in wool and in thread, workers who were employed in the dye shops and the stretching sheds, menders, sorters, shearers, beaters, combers, and weavers. These were all banded together, some nine thousand men. .... The second new guild was made up of dyers, washers, carders, and makers of combs. .... In the third guild were menders, trimmers, stretchers, washers, shirtmakers, tailors, stocking-makers, and makers of flags. .... So all together, the lower guilds increased by some thirteen thousand men.

The lord priors and the colleges decided to burn the old Communal scrutiny lists, and this was done. Then a new scrutiny was held. The Offices were divided as follows: the [seven] greater guilds had three priors; the fourteen [lower] guilds had another three, and the three new guilds had three priors. And so a new scrutiny was completed, which satisfied many who had never before had any share of the offices, and had always borne the expenses.

DOCUMENT 7

A Letter from Piero de'Medici Representing the Medici Bank in Bruges Regarding a Papal Appointment of a Bishop[7]

This letter demonstrates the Medici bank's close ties to the papacy and extensive European connections. The papacy used the Medici bank to collect the fees paid by those nominated to a bishopric. The papal bull (edict) nominating the bishop was sent to the nearest branch of the Medici bank, which would hold it until the appropriate fees were received. In this letter, Piero de'Medici, writing from Bruges, informs the archbishop of York, Cardinal John Kempe, that although King Henry VI had asked the pope to name another as bishop of London, agents of the Medici in Rome had obtained the pope's guarantee that he would appoint the archbishop's nephew Thomas Kempe. Piero informs the archbishop that his company has the bull but will be forced to send it back unless the appropriate fees are paid by the end of the month.

To my most reverend father in Christ and most fearsome lord:

After every humble recommendation, you should deign to understand that we here in the villa at Bruges have received bulls concerning Your Most Reverend Paternity pertaining to the bishopric of London; for although the lord King of England wrote to our most holy father the lord pope in order to provide someone other than you with the same bishopric, you should deign to understand that our fellow associates at the Roman Curia [i.e., the Medici *filiale* of Rome] have worked on your behalf with the lord pope so that no matter what will be written back to him concerning the aforesaid bishopric, he will not change what has been done on that account. For indeed in this our aforesaid associates carried themselves as far as they were able in such a way that, although you did not have an agent in the said Roman Curia, nevertheless your interests

---

7. From "A letter from the Medici bank in Bruges," in A. Grunzweig, *Correspondance de la filiale de Bruges des Medici* (Brussels: M. Lamertin, 1931), letter no. 8, 14–15. Translation by Kirsty Schut.

advanced so successfully that it was as if you had some agent in Rome. Furthermore, most reverend father and most fearsome lord, you should deign to know that our associates in the Roman Curia have written to us that we should conduct it so that Gierozzo de' Pigli, Florentine merchant [of the *filiale* of the Medici] in London, should be content with you and satisfied with the sums of money owed by you to our aforesaid associates by the end of the present month of December, just as our aforesaid associates, as we hope, will write to Your Most Reverend Paternity concerning these matters, in the letters of theirs that we send to you along with the present ones. Wherefore we exhort Your Most Reverend Paternity that you will deign by the end of December to pay and make satisfaction for your debts with the sums of money to the aforesaid Gierozzo de' Pigli, our associate in London, otherwise, according to the commission given to us by our aforesaid associates, it will be necessary for us to return your bulls once again to the Curia, which we would not do lightly. Your messenger who you last sent toward the Curia performed extreme diligence just as well as he ought to and was able. Most reverend father in Christ and most fearsome lord, pardon us for having written to you in such a familiar way, directing us, as the least of your servants, which Your Most Reverend Paternity knows are most ready to please, as the Highest knows. May He deign to preserve Your Most Reverend Paternity in increase of eternal beatitude. Written at Bruges on the fifth day of the month of December, 1448. The humble servants of Your Most Reverend Paternity, Piero de' Medici and Associates

DOCUMENT 8

Pius II (Aeneas Silvius Piccolomini) on Cosimo de'Medici's Character, Wealth, and Power[8]

Aeneas Silvius Piccolomini (1405–1464) was born into an ancient Sienese family and enjoyed a fine humanist education. He served as secretary to high ecclesiastics and at the Council of Basel where his rhetorical skill was noted. He became the secretary and poet laureate to the Emperor Frederick III in 1442, but in 1446 he abandoned his previously dissolute life and became a priest. His skill as a diplomat resulted in the pope appointing him a bishop and later a cardinal. In 1458 he was elected pope as Pius II. Although he encouraged humanist learning and had Bernardo Rossellino construct an ideal city (Pienza), much of his energy as pope was directed toward a crusade that would free Constantinople from the Turks. His Commentaries *is the only autobiography ever written by a reigning pope.*

Cosimo de' Medici stirred up a faction against these men and as a result was banished from the city. Uzzano was already dead and Cosimo remained in exile for some time. Then, as Pope Eugenius [IV] was holding court in Florence and various parties were contending with one another, Cosimo returned from exile. With the city in uproar, he subdued his opponents and regained his old power, driving Rodolfo and Palla and many other citizens into exile. They never returned, though Rodolfo enlisted the services of Niccolò Piccinino against his country and raided and plundered the territory of the Mugello; afterwards, however, he died in exile. Palla endured adversity cheerfully and devoted his old age to the study of philosophy at Padua, where he died at nearly ninety, a man who had not deserved the banishment imposed on him by his compatriots.

After thus disposing of his rivals, Cosimo proceeded to govern the state as he saw fit, amassing a fortune such as even Croesus could scarcely have owned. The palace he built for himself in Florence was fit for a king;

8. From Pope Pius II, *Commentaries*, vol. 1, eds. Margaret Meserve and Marcello Simonetta (Cambridge, MA: Harvard University Press, 2003), section on Cosimo, Book II, ch. 28, 314–19.

he restored a number of churches and erected others; he established the splendid monastery of San Marco and stocked its library with Greek and Latin manuscripts; he decorated his villas in magnificent style. By these noble works, it seemed that he had almost triumphed over envy, but the people will ever despise an outstanding character. There were some who claimed that Cosimo's tyranny was intolerable and tried various means to thwart his projects; some even hurled abuse at him.

At this point, it came time to assess the property of every citizen. The Florentines call this process *catasto*, the Sienese *libra*. It allows the magistrates to determine the resources of the citizenry and thus apportion levies fairly among them. Cosimo was in favor of a new catasto; his opponents were against it. Therefore it was decided to call a general meeting of the city. As the people were assembling, a group of armed men gathered from all quarters at Cosimo's command; they surrounded the piazza and made it clear that anyone who objected to Cosimo's plans did so at his peril. The catasto was approved under threat of violence; some of the citizens who had opposed it were banished and others were fined.

After this Cosimo was refused nothing. In matters of war and peace his decisions were final and his word was regarded as law, not so much a citizen as the master of his city. Government meetings were held at his house; his candidates were elected to public office; he enjoyed every semblance of royal power except a title and a court. It was for this reason that, when Pius asked the bishop of Orte what he thought about Florence and he replied that it was a pity so beautiful a woman had no husband, the pope said, "Yes, but she has a lover," meaning that she had a tyrant instead of a king. Pius was referring to Cosimo who, as an illegitimate lord, kept the city and its people in cruel servitude. During Pius's stay in Florence, Cosimo was ill or rather (as many believed) he pretended to be ill, so he would not have to wait on the pope.

Cosimo's ancestors came to Florence from the Mugello. His father Giovanni became a client of the Medici and took the name of the family. He left an enormous fortune to his sons, Cosimo and Lorenzo, which grew incredibly in Cosimo's hands. His business interests ranged over all of Europe and he traded as far as Egypt. He was of fine physique and more than average height; his countenance and speech were mild; he was more cultured than merchants usually are and had some knowledge of Greek; his mind was keen and alert to everything going on around him; his spirit was neither cowardly nor rash; he easily endured toil and hunger and often went whole nights without sleep. Nothing happened in Italy without his knowledge; indeed it was his advice that guided the policy of many cities and princes. Nor were foreign events a secret to him, for his business contacts all over the world sent him a constant stream of letters which kept him abreast of affairs in their states. Toward the end of his life he suffered from gout, a disease which he lived to see his sons and grandsons inherit. When the pope passed through Florence he was more than seventy years old.

DOCUMENT 9

Leonardo Bruni's Praise of the City of Florence[9]

Leonardo Bruni (c. 1370–1444) was born in Arezzo but moved to Florence where he entered the circle of the humanist chancellor Coluccio Salutati. He also served as a papal secretary in Rome before his election as Florentine chancellor from 1427 to 1444. In that office he articulated the ideals of civic humanism and wrote his celebrated History of the Florentine People *and a great many other seminal humanist texts. His* Laudatio florentinae urbis *(Praise of the City of Florence) was a panegyric written about 1404 and was derived from the ancient* Panathenaic Oration *of Aelius Aristides.*

I wish that God immortal would bestow upon me an eloquence worthy of the city of Florence, of which I am about to speak, or at least an eloquence that equals my love and zeal for it. One form of eloquence or the other would, I believe, suffice in revealing the magnificence and splendor of this city. Nothing more beautiful or more splendid than Florence can be found anywhere in the world. I must confess that I have never been more willing to undertake anything than the present task. I have no doubt whatsoever that if my wish for either type of eloquence were granted, I would be able to describe this illustrious and beautiful city in an articulate and dignified manner. Since, however, not all our wishes can be fulfilled, I shall do my best, thereby showing that I was lacking not in will, but rather in talent.

The splendor of this city is so remarkable that no eloquence could begin to describe it. We know that a number of distinguished and righteous men have dared speak about God Himself, whose glory and infinite nature a man's words, no matter how eloquent they may be, can never come close to capturing; but regardless of God's ineffable superiority, they still attempt to employ all their rhetorical skills in speaking about such infinitude. I, on the other hand, shall have fulfilled my task

9. From Leonardo Bruni, *Laudatio Urbis Florentinae*, in *Images of Quattrocento Florence: Selected Writings in Literature, History, and Art*, eds. S. Baldassarri and A. Saiber (New Haven: Yale University Press, 2000), 40–43.

of praising Florence if I make adequate use of all the knowledge I have acquired through my ardent study, although I know full well that my ability cannot ultimately apprehend such an extraordinary city.

I now must face something most orators face, namely, that they do not know where to begin their speech. In my case, however, this is not owing to a lack of words, but to the subject matter itself—and not only because of the many things that are relevant to one another, but also because they are all so remarkable that they seem to compete for excellence among themselves. It is, thus, not easy to decide which topic should be discussed first. If you consider the beauty and the magnificence of the city, you would think that there is nothing more deserving with which to begin a speech. If, on the other hand, you take into account its power and wealth, you would think it right to start an oration with these topics. Furthermore, if you look at its deeds both in the present and in the past, nothing could appear more important than to begin here. But if you focus on its customs and institutions, nothing could seem more worthy of distinction. With all this to think about I am uncertain where to begin; and when I am about to commence with a certain topic, another catches my attention and I cannot resolve which to discuss first. Nonetheless, I shall begin at what I find to be the most logical starting point, although I do not consider the other subjects less worthy of attention.

As it sometimes happens that a son's resemblance to his parents is immediately noticeable, so the Florentines resemble their most noble and illustrious city to such a degree that one is led to believe that they could have never lived anywhere else, nor could Florence ever have had any other kind of inhabitants. Just as these citizens far excel all other people by virtue of their natural genius, prudence, wealth, and magnificence, so Florence, whose site was most carefully chosen, is superior to all others in splendor, beauty, and cleanliness.

First of all, let us note the signs of its wisdom. For one, Florence has never done anything ostentatiously; it has always preferred to reject dangerous and foolish arrogance in order to pursue a state of peace and tranquility. It was not built on top of a mountain, to show off its greatness; nor, by the same token, was it built in the middle of a plain and open on all sides to attack. Instead, with the discerning prudence of its citizens, Florence attained the best of both situations. They [the Florentines] knew that it was impossible to live on mountaintops without being subjected to the harshness of the elements—strong winds and heavy rains—which are uncomfortable and hazardous to the inhabitants. They also recognized that a city placed in the middle of plains, correspondingly, is necessarily disturbed by the dampness of the soil, the impurity of the air, and fog. Attempting to avoid all these risks, and acting as wisely as always, they built Florence midway between the two extremes: it lies far from the discomforts of the mountains and free, at the same time, from the inconveniences of the plains. It has the best of both situations, and a good climate, too. To the north, the mountains of Fiesole, like a kind of fortification, ward off severe cold and the furious gusts of northern winds. To the south, smaller hills protect it from the less violent winds that blow from that direction. In the other areas surrounding the city are sunny fields open to gentle breezes. Florence sits peacefully in an ideal location and climate; when you move away from it in any direction, you will meet with more severe cold or more intense sun.

From the hills to the plains, moreover, the entire city is surrounded by a splendid circuit of walls which are not so excessively imposing to make it appear fearful and dubious of its power; nor, on the other hand, are they so small or neglected to give the impression of being conceited or indiscreet. And what can I say of the multitude of inhabitants, of the splendid buildings, of the richly decorated churches, of the incredible wealth of the whole city? Everything here, by Jove, is astonishingly beautiful....

DOCUMENT 10

Timoteo Maffei's Defense of Cosimo's Patronage[10]

Timoteo Maffei (c. 1415–1470) was a prior of St. John Lateran, Rome's cathedral, and from 1467 the bishop of Ragusa (Dubrovnik) in Dalmatia. He received a humanist education under Guarino da Verona and taught theology at Padua. A close friend of Cosimo de'Medici and instrumental in Cosimo's rebuilding the Badia Fiesolana (1462), Timoteo composed this dialogue between 1454 and 1456 in response to certain "detractors" who questioned Cosimo's motives and "excess."

Granted, perhaps someone like you will censure Cosimo for excess since he will have seen the monastery of San Marco, built at his own expense, not only of such size but also ornament, and within enclosed a multitude of books, as well as with quantities of sacred vestments, silver plate or with the splendour of gold, such as the vows of poor religious do not seem to require. Perhaps another will reproach him since he [Cosimo] recently began to renovate his residence. He will have seen the highest and widest walls in remarkable stony order, the more thick and lofty columns, the marble statues, the remarkable paintings which you would attribute to Apelles or Lysippos, the most well-equipped bedrooms of the sons of Piero and Giovanni, sundials decorated in gold, and etched with wonderful variety, stools of cyprus, and other things which seem more appropriate to a Prince than to a private citizen. Others perhaps will criticize the church of the Martyr Laurence because he undertook it at such expense and with so many embellishments that the work of no King in our day may be compared with it. Yet all these things are worthy of extraordinary praise, and deserve to be entrusted to posterity with the greatest enthusiasm since in the building of monasteries and churches Cosimo's Magnificence had divine excellence before its eyes, and it devised them not with respect to the religious or clergy, but with how much devotion to God and with what degree of thanksgiving we ought

10. From Timoteo Maffei, *On the Magnificence of Cosimo de'Medici of Florence against [his] Detractors*, in Peter Howard, *Creating Magnificence in Renaissance Florence* (Toronto: Centre for Reformation and Renaissance Studies, 2012), 142–43.

to enjoy them. Moreover, in [the construction of] his house Cosimo has considered not what may be appropriate to himself but to Florence, such a great city and of such a size. As many more benefits were bestowed by the city on him than on all the rest of the citizenry, lest he should seem ungrateful, he conferred ampler and more brilliant embellishments on it than had others. Certainly, we see in this time his tendency to do so in a marvellous way. A testimony of this relevant to what we have been talking about is also that structure which they call a Dormitory, and which he erected for the young brothers in the most spacious Monastery of Santa Croce, whose cells are embellished and reinforced with ornamentation or furniture of some sort—a matter of which I do not speak easily. And for the observant friars of Blessed Francis he built, from the ground up and completed in every part, a Monastery in a field in the Mugello, for which I do not know what could be thought more suitable or more pious, both by the nature of the place and the workmanship. About one thousand five hundred paces from this city at a place called Carreggi, he has renovated a house worthy of any city at such great expense, and to the great astonishment of all, so that in everyone's judgement there is no one more blessed than he as regards magnificence of works. These things compel me both to admire and then to recommend this man wholeheartedly, and to exhort others so that they may acclaim [him].

DOCUMENT 11

The Plot against Piero di Cosimo, 1466, Described in the Diary of Luca Landucci[11]

Luca Landucci (1436–1516) was a Florentine apothecary who owned a druggist's shop in central Florence. In 1450, he began a diary that recorded those events in Florence that he thought newsworthy. After his death in 1516 the diary was continued anonymously until 1542.

1st September [1466] I bought the apothecary's shop at the *Canto de' Tornaquinci*; and took over the keys on the 4th.

On this day a *parlamento* (assembly) was held in the Piazza, and there was a great commotion in the city; the shops were closed several times, for fear that they might be looted. Niccolò Soderini, Messer Dietisalvi, and Messer Luca Pitti were exiled, for having been the leaders in the plot against Piero, son of Cosimo de'Medici, when it was attempted to murder him in his way from Careggi. And after the failure of the plot, many citizens connected with it were exiled, about twenty-seven of them being restricted within certain boundaries and made ineligible for office, according to the sentences inscribed on a document inserted in this book; except Messer Luca Pitti, who made an alliance with Giovanni Tornabuoni, giving him his daughter as wife, and in consequence he was reprieved from exile, and they remained friends and at peace.

---

11. Luca Landucci, *A Florentine Diary from 1450 to 1516*, trans. Alicia de Rosen Jervis (London: J. M. Dent and Sons, 1927), 8.

DOCUMENT 12

A Letter from Lucrezia Tornabuoni to Her Husband, Piero, Discussing a Prospective Bride for Their Son Lorenzo[12]

Lucrezia Tornabuoni (1427–1482) was born in Florence to the powerful Tornabuoni family and married Piero di Cosimo de'Medici in 1444. She was an important patron of religious institutions and the arts, as well as a writer of religious poetry and plays. After the death of Piero, she was a powerful influence on her son Lorenzo the Magnificent and served as his adviser in a great many areas. She was also a skilled businesswoman, acquiring property and making successful investments. Much of her wealth she used, however, for charity, especially in assisting widows and orphan girls.

In this letter Lorenzo's mother writes to her husband, Piero de'Medici, from Rome, describing a prospective bride for their son Lorenzo. In 1469, Clarice Orsini (1450–1488) and Lorenzo de'Medici were indeed married.

Along the way I wrote to you often, telling you about the roads we took to get here. I arrived Thursday and was received by Giovanni [Tornabuoni, her brother and manager of the Rome branch of the Medici bank] with great delight as you can imagine. I received your letter of the 21st, and it relieved me greatly to learn that you are no longer in pain. Nonetheless, every day seems like a year until I return, both for your consolation and for my own.

Thursday morning, going to St. Peter's I met Maddalena Orsini, the cardinal's sister; she had with her daughter [Clarice], who is fifteen or sixteen years old. She was dressed in the Roman fashion, with a draped shawl, and dressed like that she seemed very lovely to me, fair and tall, but since the girl was covered up I could not see her as well as I would have liked. Yesterday, as it happened, I went to visit Monsignor Orsini, mentioned above, in his sister's home, which adjoins his. After I greeted

12. From Lisa Kaborycha, ed. and trans., *A Corresponding Renaissance: Letters Written by Italian Women, 1375–1650* (Oxford: Oxford University Press, 2016), 106–8.

him and paid my respects to his Lordship on your behalf, the sister unexpectedly appeared with the said girl, this time wearing a tight skirt in the Roman style, but without the shawl. We stayed quite a while talking together and I was able to study the girl closely. As I have said, she is of acceptable height and has fair skin; she has a sweet manner, but is not as well-bred as our girls; however, she displays great modesty and will soon learn our customs. She is not blond, because they are not like that here; her red hair, of which there is plenty, hangs loose. Her face is a little on the round side, but it does not displease me. Her neck is suitably slender, but seems to me a little thin, or rather delicate. We could not see her bust, because it is the custom here to go around all covered up, but it seems to be of good quality. She goes around with her head not held high like our girls, but she carries it a little forward, and this I believe is due to her embarrassment, for I see no reason for her posture other than that. Her hands are long and slender, and all in all, we judge her to be above average, although not to be compared with Maria, Lucrezia, and Bianca [Lucrezia and Piero's daughters]. Lorenzo himself has seen her; you will learn yourself whether he is content. Whatever you and he decide will be fine and I will go along with it. May God guide you to make the best choice.

The girl's father is Jacopo Orsini of Monterotondo, and her mother is the sister of the cardinal. She has two brothers, one is a man of arms, who is held in high esteem by Signor Orso; the other is a subdeacon priest of the pope. They have one half of Monterotondo, the other half belongs to their uncle, who has two sons and three daughters. They have, in addition to this half of Monterotondo, three other castles, belonging to her brothers, and as far as I can learn they are well off, and doing ever better, for, besides being nephews of the cardinal, the archbishop, Napoleon, and the knight, through their mother, they are also cousins through their father's side since the girl's father is second cousin in direct line of the aforesaid lords, who love him dearly. And this is what I have been able to describe. If before setting the thing in motion you wanted to await our return, do as you see fit.

I am thinking of leaving here on Monday the 8th, taking the road that you know of and will be there at the arranged time. May God in His Grace conduct us safely home and keep you in good health. I am not writing to Monna Contessina [her mother-in-law, Cosimo's widow], since it does not seem necessary. Commend me to her and send the girls my greetings as well as Lorenzo and Giuliano. In Rome, on the 28th of March, 1467

Your Lucrezia.

DOCUMENT 13

Tumult in Florence, 1470, from a Letter from Alessandra Strozzi to Her Son Filippo, in Naples[13]

Alessandra Macinghi Strozzi (c. 1408–1471) was a Florentine patrician whose husband Matteo's family, the Strozzi, belonged to the Oligarchical faction opposed to the Medici; consequently, Matteo and several of her children went into exile. After Matteo's death in 1435, Alessandra returned to Florence. Her sons, including Filippo, the recipient of this letter, were accepted into the bank run by Matteo's cousins, which had branches in Bruges, Barcelona, and Naples; Filippo founded his own bank and cloth warehouse in Naples with his brother, Lorenzo. Although both brothers were formally exiled from Florence as opponents of the Medici in 1458, Alessandra remained to manage the family property and attend to the interests of her children. Over seventy of her letters survive, providing an important insight into fifteenth-century Florentine life.

[. . .] You'll have heard the news from here. First, there have been two attempts to break out of the Stinche, that is, the prison. The first time, they broke the windows and got out into the courtyard before being recaptured, and then pardoned. The second time, they burned the prison gates and broke down the wall at the same place where Matteo di Giorgio tried to escape: but they didn't succeed, because they were heard, and the soldiers who are in the Piazza came running, and used their crossbows to shoot at one man who was trying to get out through the gaps. Then they were recaptured, and three of them were beheaded, and the others were put back in prison. Then, on the 6th of this month, in the morning at the fourteenth hour, news came that that man from the Nardi family had entered Prato with no fewer than two hundred infantry, and that Prato was lost. Oh, don't ask what an upheaval there was here in the city! For two hours, the streets were full of a mass of people running hither and thither, and particularly in the street where Lorenzo di Piero [de'Medici]

---

13. From Alessandra Macinghi Strozzi, *Letters to Her Sons (1447–1470)*, ed. and trans. Judith Bryce (Toronto: Iter Academic Press, 2016), 242–44 (no. 72).

lives; and whatever baked bread could be found was all carried off, either to his house or to the palace [of the Signoria], so that there was no bread or flour to be had. I thought I was going to be badly off, because I haven't any grain in the house, and not much flour. Then, by the grace of God, news came that this Nardi had been taken prisoner, along with all his men—they say there were about sixty of them—and the same day he was led away captive. Then the following day, the 7th, fifteen of them came, all bound with a rope: and on Monday, which was the 9th, Nardi had his head cut off, and the same day, three other men, also from Prato, were taken prisoner. And it's said in Prato that the podestà had fourteen men hanged. Then this morning, four were hanged; and they say seven more will be hanged next Monday. I don't know what will happen to the rest. The people have all had a great fright: it seems a dreadful thing to happen, with so many people killed and tortured. And on top of this tribulation, there have been earthquakes; and on the morning that poor man entered Prato, there was a really big one. What with one fright and the other, I'm half out of mind: and I think the world is coming to an end, so it's a good idea to make one's peace with God, and to be prepared. May he preserve us from any more such tribulations. I also hear that something or other has happened in Pistoia, and people are saying that the Panciatichi there have all fled in panic. Please God there's an end to all this. No more for now. God keep you from harm. From your Alessandra Strozzi, in Florence.

DOCUMENT 14

Lorenzo de' Medici, the Magnificent, on His Expenses[14]

The Medici used their wealth to reinforce their position in the city among all classes of citizens. Here, Lorenzo the Magnificent revealed the huge sums spent on everything from sponsoring lavish public spectacles, like jousts, to commissioning buildings and giving alms to the poor.

[1469] To do as others had done, I held a joust in the Piazza S. Croce at great expense and with great pomp. I find we spent about 10,000 ducats. ... Piero, our father, departed this life on July 2 ... having been much tormented with gout. He would not make a will, but we drew up an inventory and found we possessed 237,988 scudi [a coin worth approximately a florin]. ...

I find that from 1434 till now we have spent large sums of money, as appear in a small quarto notebook of the said year to the end of 1471. Incredible are the sums written down. They amount to 663,755 florins for alms, buildings, and taxes, let alone other expenses. But I do not regret this, for though many would consider it better to have a part of that sum in their purse, I consider that it gave great honor to our State, and I think the money was well expended, and am well pleased.

---

14. From Brucker, ed., *The Society of Renaissance Florence*, doc. 15, 27.

DOCUMENT 15

The Sack of Volterra as Witnessed by an Exiled Volterran Poet[15]

Little is known about Giovanni di Antonio Zacchi other than his position as one of the twelve men elected by the General Council of Volterra to determine Volterran policy regarding the dispute with Florence over the alum mines.

I.

No massacre greater than that of Troy,
    a vaster and more extended ruin
    ever was heard of, since the summit of Ilion [Troy]
    when it fell into the hands of the Greeks.

An infamous event, memorable and strange,
    a horrible example of our lives,
    so that it still brings me to tears
    —and now that of my Volterran people,

torn to pieces by the rabid lion,
    and plundered by the Florentines,
    in the harsh yoke of their plight.

Dispersed were my citizens
    in fourteen hundred seventy-two,
    ploughing the world in different realms.

---

15. From Giovanni Zacchi Volterrano, *Sonnets on the Sack of Volterra*, in Biagio Lisci, ed., *Il sacco di Volterra nel MCDLXXII: poesie storiche contemporanee e commentario inedito* (Bologna: G. Gomagnoli, 1886), 67–68. Translated by Kirsty Schut.

II.

I, a wanderer, placed under a haughty yoke
    walk alpine hills, thorny mountains,
    deep, dark valleys, fearsome bridges,
    high rocks, a wild and bramble covered path,

a thunderous cave, a black forest,
    torrid rivers and resounding springs,
    through beeches and firs almost touching the sky,
    barbarous people, of austere custom and dress,

by means of Aeolus [the Greek god of the winds] raging
that at such a time
    I fly to carve in stone one land in another,
    through dense fog and washed-out slopes.

It is not always that at every moment and hour
    I remember and weep for that land
    where I left my divine phoenix.

        I speak of Volterra,
that sends me, an exile, to wander throughout the world,
bearing the weight of others' crimes.

DOCUMENT 16

Angelo Poliziano's Description of the Pazzi Conspiracy[16]

Angelo Poliziano (Angelo Ambrogini, 1454–1494; his popular name comes from his home city of Montepulciano) was a classical scholar, leading humanist, and close associate of the Medici, serving as the tutor to Lorenzo's sons and participating in the informal Platonic academy where he formed a deep friendship with Pico della Mirandola. His Commentarium *was composed almost immediately after the Pazzi Conspiracy, with the aim of depicting the Medici as innocent victims. It is thus a work of propaganda as well as history.*

I am resolved to describe briefly the Pazzi Conspiracy, a crime most worthy of record that occurred in my own times, for indeed it almost overthrew the whole Florentine public from within.

The state of this city was then that while all the good people were on the side of the brothers Lorenzo and Giuliano and the rest of the Medici family, a branch of the Pazzi family and some of the Salviati began, first in secret and then even openly, to oppose the existing government. They envied the power of the Medici family in public affairs and its brilliance in private ones, and they sought to destroy it as much as they could.

[...]

The Medici family was splendid and magnificent in all their undertakings, especially in receiving famous personages. No famous man either came to Florence or Florentine territory whom that household did not treat with this sort of magnificence. When, therefore, as soon as Cardinal Raffaello, the son of Count Girolamo's sister, had arrived at Jacopo's country villa outside the city, where, we have shown, the conspiracy was planned, the conspirators seized the opportunity for the evil deed. They announced the cardinal to the brothers so that they might receive him at their villa in Fiesole. There Lorenzo and I, with his son Piero, went;

---

16. From Angelo Poliziano, *Pactianae coniurationis commentarium,* selections on the Pazzi Conspiracy, trans. Elizabeth B. Welles, in *The Earthly Republic: Italian Humanists on Government and Society,* ed. Benjamin G. Kohl and Ronald G. Witt (Philadelphia: University of Pennsylvania Press, 1978), 305–22.

Giuliano stayed home because he was hindered by the state of his health, which delayed the matter to the day that we have mentioned. Then they wrote anew [to Lorenzo] more familiarly, that the Cardinal very much wanted to be received at a banquet in Florence to see the ornaments of the palace; the hangings, tapestries, gems, silver, and all the other precious objects. The two excellent young men suspected no trickery; they prepared the house; they got out the ornaments, spread out the tapestries, arranged the silver, statues, and paintings for public view, put out the gems in their cases, and had a most magnificent banquet prepared.

And then, before long, the conspirators began to ask where Lorenzo and Giuliano were. They found out that they had both gone to Santa Reparata [the old name of Florence's cathedral], so they hurried off. The Cardinal was led, according to custom, onto a platform in the choir. While the Eucharist was being celebrated, the archbishop, along with Jacopo di Poggio [son of the humanist chancellor Poggio Bracciolini], the two Jacopo Salviati, and several companions, went to the Palazzo Vecchio in order to throw the rulers of Florence out of their citadel and take over the palace. The rest stayed in the church to carry out their evil work. Although assigned to Lorenzo's murder, Giovanni Battista had withdrawn from the crime, and Antonio da Volterra had taken it over; the rest were attending to Giuliano.

As soon as the communion of the priest was over and the signal had been given, Bernardo Bandini, Francesco Pazzi, and other conspirators surrounded Giuliano in a circle. First Bandini struck the young man, forcing his sword through his chest. Giuliano, dying, fled a few steps; they followed. Gasping for breath the youth fell to the ground. Francesco stabbed him again and again with his dagger. Thus this upright young man was murdered. His servant, breathless with terror, flung himself into hiding in a most contemptible fashion.

Meanwhile, the chosen assassins attacked Lorenzo, and Antonio, first laying a hand on his left shoulder, aimed his dagger at Lorenzo's throat. The latter, undaunted, let his mantel fall and wrapped it around his left arm, drawing his sword out of its scabbard at the same time; however, he received one more blow, and, as he freed himself, was wounded in the neck. Then, as a man both astute and brave, he turned upon his murderers with his unsheathed sword, watching carefully and guarding himself. They were terrified and took flight while his two courtiers, Andrea and Lorenzo Cavalcanti, were quick to defend him. Lorenzo was wounded in the arm; Andrea came through safely.

The panic of the people was something to be seen: men, women, and children fleeing everywhere, wherever their feet took them. The whole place was filled with roaring and groaning, yet you could not hear anything that was said, and there were some who thought the church would collapse.

[...]

Meanwhile the Archbishop of Pisa called Cesare Petrucci, the Gonfaloniere of Justice, as they say, into council, so that he could kill him, although he said he had something to tell him from the Pope. Certain of the exiles from Perugia who accompanied him into the Palazzo Vecchio knew about the evil affair. They met in the chancellery so they would hold an advantageous position, but when they closed the doors of the room, they could not open them when it was necessary; thus they were no help either to themselves or to their own side. But Petrucci, as he gazed to the faltering Salviati, suspected the plot and called the guards to arms. Salviati, much upset and scared, rushed out of the room, whereupon Petrucci met up with Jacopo di Poggio and with great courage grabbed him by the hair, threw him to the ground, and called guards to watch him. Then he ran hastily into the high tower of the palazzo with a band of all of the magistrates. There, as best he could, he guarded the doors with a spit snatched from the kitchen (fear and anger had provided him with this weapon) and fiercely defended his own and the public safety. The others fought likewise bravely for their lives. The Palazzo Vecchio has numerous doors, and these were closed by guards so that the chiefs of the conspirators were separated. Thus divided, they lost much of the momentum of their attack. Meanwhile, there was a low murmuring noise throughout the Palazzo where some of the citizens had gathered.

[...]

Meanwhile, Lorenzo's sympathizers regained the Palazzo Vecchio. The Perugian conspirators broke down their door and were slaughtered. In this way the Medici supporters vented their rage upon the rest. They hanged Jacopo di Poggi from the windows; they led the captive cardinal to the Palazzo with a large guard and had much difficulty in protecting him from an attack by the people. Most of those who followed him were killed by the crowd, all torn apart, their bodies mangled cruelly; in front of Lorenzo's doors someone brought, now a head fixed on a spear, now a shoulder. Nothing else was heard besides the voices of the people shouting "Palle, Palle"—for that is the Medici insignia.

But Jacopo Pazzi decided to take flight, and with an armed band he made for the Porta alla Croce and escaped.

The people, meanwhile, were gathering at the Medici palace with incredible excitement and demonstration of support. They demanded that the traitors be handed over to them for punishment and spared no threat or abuse until they forced the criminals to be arrested. The house of Jacopo Pazzi was barely defended from plunder, and Francesco, naked and wounded, was taken almost half dead to the hangman by the company of Pietro Corsini; for it was not easy, or even possible, to control the fury of the crowd. From the same window as Francesco Pazzi, the archbishop of Pisa was also hanged directly above the dead body itself. When he had been cut down (I witnessed in the amazed faces of the crowd what happened, and it was unknown to none at the time), either by chance or anger he bit Francesco's corpse in the chest, and even as he was strangled with the noose, his eyes wide open in rage, he hung onto it with his teeth. After this the necks of the two Jacopos Salviati were broken by hanging.

I remember that I came then into the piazza (for things were quiet now at the Medici palace), where I saw many corpses strewn about, foully mangled and greatly mocked and scorned by the people, for the House of the Medici had earned the gratitude of the people for many reasons. Everyone abhorred the death of Giuliano, calling the crime unworthy of such an excellent young man; the darling of the Florentine youth was the last person who should have been killed by plotting, trickery, and treason, and that such a crime should have been committed by a family both violent and sacrilegious, detested by God and man alike. . . .

DOCUMENT 17

Marsilio Ficino Writes a Consoling Letter to Lorenzo de'Medici in the Aftermath of Pazzi Conspiracy[17]

Marsilio Ficino (1433–1499), humanist philosopher, astrologer, priest, physician, and mystic, was the son of Cosimo de'Medici's physician. Cosimo engaged the young Ficino to translate the known works of Plato from Greek into Latin and in 1462 gave him use of a villa at Careggi as a place to live and work. Besides his Latin texts of Plato, Ficino translated the Hermetic Books and other mystical texts, including those of the Pseudo-Dionysius. It was around Ficino that the informal gatherings of the Platonic academy occurred under Lorenzo de'Medici. Ficino believed that Platonism and Christianity could be reconciled, and his major work, the Theologia Platonica, *attempted to reveal the essential truths of both. He was initially sympathetic to Savonarola but soon distanced himself, unlike his friend and fellow Platonist, Pico della Mirandola.*

Marsilio Ficino to Lorenzo de' Medici: greetings.

Long ago, Lorenzo, I heard that men of evil conduct were utterly distasteful to you, and recently I have heard that good men approve of you precisely because you disapprove of evil men. For the one I thoroughly commend you, and for the other I heartily congratulate you. For there is no shorter, no easier way to the good than to hate evil; no surer sign of good taste than to reject those tastes which are harmful to health. There is no life more secure, no surer glory, than to be loved by good and discerning men; for even the wicked are finally compelled to honour those loved by the upright and discerning. Yet in order that evil men may not only be hateful to you but fill you with horror, I wish, if I may, to observe for a while the utterly repulsive and wretched life of those ruled by passion and, as it were, to point it out to you.

---

17. From *The Letters of Marsilio Ficino*, trans. School of Economic Science Language Department, ed. Clement Salaman (London: Shepheard Walwyn Publishers, 1994), vol. 5, letter 44, 67–69.

Lorenzo, the soul corrupted by evil conduct is like a wood dense with tangled thorns, bristling with savage beasts, infested with poisonous snakes. Or it is like a swelling sea, tossed by battling winds, waves and wild storms; or like a human body misshapen without and tortured within by excruciating pains in every joint. On the other hand, a mind endued with fine principles is like a well-tended and fertile field, or a calm and peaceful sea, or the body of a man which is both beautiful and strong.

My friend, we have now seen the shadow of the evil mind and its opposite, the image of the good mind. As soon as we perceive the first clearly, we cannot but loathe it; but when we see the second, we cannot but love and venerate it. How else can one become a good man except by resolutely seeking the company of a mind that is good and shunning one that is evil?

In the same way as we have been considering the evil soul and the good soul, please tell me, excellent Lorenzo, do you now wish to look more closely with me into the ignorant mind and into the mind that has been enlightened? I believe you do desire this very strongly, and I, for my part, wish to show it to you briefly. The mind ignorant of truth is just like the moon when the earth is between it and the sun and it undergoes an eclipse: it is deprived of the sun's splendour. Or again, it is like the cold and foggy air of night, or like a human body with blind eyes, deaf ears, and mute tongue. On the other hand, we can compare the mind which has knowledge of reality and the full power of speech, to the full moon shining in the light of the sun, or to the clear air of day with its abundant light and gentle warmth, or to the body whose senses are alert and whose tongue is free to speak. But whoever sees the mind ignorant of truth and does not flee immediately from its foul appearance or shadow, will flee from nothing; while whoever does not eagerly follow the mind which does not know the truth, wherever such a mind appears, will not, I see, follow anything anywhere.

So press on, my Lorenzo, press on, I beg you. Flee, as you once began to, far from that loathsome shadow, from that miserable image of the impure and ignorant mind. Bestir yourself, and every day with all your strength pursue more and more closely, as you do, the form of the good and wise soul, full of light and bliss. Just as nature endowed you at birth and fortune enriched you thereafter, may you by your own efforts enrich yourself in the same measure, so that you may not consider yourself lacking in anything; for nature as well as fortune has provided you with everything else that you could wish for. All your possessions—your lands, houses, furnishings, clothes and even the limbs of your body—shine around you, each of them, like stars. May you also shine out like the Sun itself amongst those stars, with your soul resplendent in the radiance of your actions and your writings.

DOCUMENT 18

An Allegory of Lorenzo the Magnificent and Florence by Luca Pulci[18]

Luca Pulci (1431–1470) was a prominent Florentine poet, who often celebrated the Medici in his vernacular poems. Driadeo, *composed about 1464–1465, tells the story of a satyr's love for a nymph. Pulci flattered the Medici family by setting the poem in the Mugello, where the Medici family originated. Lorenzo appears as a character (here called "Lauro"), who holds a poetic contest with a shepherd to win the love of a nymph named Esturia [Etruria, or Tuscany?]. Here he tells Esturia about Florence.*

Book 3

(79) Lauro spoke thus: "My beautiful nymph, I wish you to dwell with me in the city that is queen of all other cities, enriched by property and castles, a university, a seaport, and divine liberty. Inhabited by a great people, it boasts experts in many arts and is perfect in all respects. I shall now briefly describe her seven virtues to you.

(80) "While on a rock by the river, you may happen to see fish in the waves, Clymene crying, and wild beasts fleeing from bold hunters in the environs of the city and within the circle of walls. My city has a worthy, noble, and undefeated people, civilized and pious, hostile to all crime. The citizens unite to protect their beloved country and travel the world over.

(81) "Its countryside is fertile and rich, dotted with villas and sacred temples. The vines of Minerva and Bacchus cover the soil, a soil which also abounds in other fruits, woods, and springs and has a temperate climate. Ceres lavishes food on the inhabitants of this region. Here you will find a variety of plants and all sorts of orchards, fine gardens, and sweet-scented flowers.

(82) "The greatest eloquence could not help me recount to you these people's skills, nor the means of becoming rich that they have discovered.

---

18. From Luca Pulci, excerpt from *Driadeo*, in *Images of Quattrocento Florence*, 89–90.

Some of them make a living by working iron, others weave clothes; no one dares waste time. Neither Daedalus nor the men who first breasted the waves aboard the Argus—not even their very captain—could be deemed as illustrious as these citizens.

(83) "This entire city espouses, like a creed, noble, sincere, and untainted liberty. It fosters sacred orders and just laws; it sentences convicts to death and banishes forgers, blasphemers, and thieves. By contrast, it rewards the worthy with appointments and high offices. It elevates the humble and answers their prayers, repays good deeds and punishes evil.

(84) "Here you will find an academy, a circle of bucolic poets who read verses from manuscripts, and schools of moral philosophers and Stoics. Cosmographers draw maps of the whole universe, while geometers elaborate precise rules. There are grammarians, orators, and historians, as well as musicians, those who track the motion of the stars, and doctors and surgeons to heal the body.

(85) "Often you will see, immediately upon their arrival at the city gates, distinguished visitors, sovereign pontiffs, and emperors being welcomed amid great joy by all the conscript fathers, our senators, and parades with princes, lords, knights, soldiers, standard-bearers, heralds, and jugglers.

(86) "You will also see the beautiful sandy river which flows through the city, where goods are loaded to be taken to the seaport. You will see men who, leaving their wives and homes, put all their merchandise on board to sail to a distant island, always consulting the North Star in tracing their route. They do not linger in seaports during their voyage; some return, some do not, as Fortune wills.

(87) "Various instruments and bells within the city mark the hours and beat the time of everyday life. One can hear diverse and praiseworthy things: some explain God's actions to the common people, clarifying their meaning; the lawyer explicates the case to his customer in great detail; others compose verses to the sound of a lyre and sing of poets, the philosophic life, and prophets.

(88) "Our holy temples and sacred oracles are open to the faithful, to heretics, and Jews; they are without any restriction whatsoever. Both laymen and priests piously attend church services, their devotion strengthened by the many miracles they witness. The floors are inlaid with porphyry, the vaults with mosaics: all the heavenly signs are painted there, from Taurus to the other ten, and Gemini too.

(89) "In beautiful, lavish, and grand palaces, I shall introduce you to the most distinguished citizens. All your commands will be fulfilled, just speak and you will see. You will wear oriental gems and golden jewels and taste the most exotic food. Is there more? Happy in our heavenly choir, from balconies and within theaters you will watch game, festivities, tournaments, and jousts."

DOCUMENT 19

Lorenzo de'Medici Writes a Letter to His Son Giovanni on Becoming a Cardinal[19]

Giovanni di Lorenzo de'Medici (1475–1521) was the second son of Lorenzo de'Medici and Clarice Orsini. He was elevated to the Sacred College in 1489 at the age of fourteen. In 1513, at the age of thirty-seven, he would be elected pope and rule as Pope Leo X until his early death in 1521.

You, and all of us who are interested in your welfare, ought to esteem ourselves highly favored by Providence, not only for the many honors and benefits bestowed upon our house, but more particularly for having conferred upon us, in your person, the greatest dignity we have ever enjoyed. This favor, in itself so important, is rendered still more so by the circumstances with which it is accompanied, and especially by the consideration of your youth and of our situation in the world. The first that I would therefore suggest to you is that you ought to be grateful to God, and continually to recollect that it is not through your merits, your prudence, or your solicitude, that this event has taken place, but through his favor, which you can only repay by a pious, chaste and exemplary life; and that your obligations to the performance of these duties are so much the greater, as in your early years you have given some reasonable expectations that your riper age may produce such fruits. It would indeed be highly disgraceful, and as contrary to your duty as to my hopes, if, at a time when others display a greater share of reason and adopt a better mode of life, you should forget the precepts of your youth, and forsake the path in which you have hitherto trodden. Endeavor, therefore, to alleviate the burden of your early dignity by the regularity of your life and by your perseverance in those studies which are suitable to your profession. It gave me great satisfaction to learn, that, in the course of the past year, you had frequently, of your own accord, gone to communion and

19. From *The letter of Lorenzo de'Medici to his son Giovanni*, in *Source-Book of the Italian Renaissance*, trans. Merrick Whitcomb (Philadelphia: University of Pennsylvania Press, 1903), 82–86.

confession; nor do I conceive that there is any better way of obtaining the favor of heaven than by habituating yourself to a performance of these and similar duties. This appears to me to be the most suitable and useful advice which, in the first instance, I can possibly give you.

I well know that as you are now to reside in Rome, that sink of all iniquity, the difficulty of conducting yourself by these admonitions will be increased. The influence of example is itself prevalent; but you will probably meet with those who will particularly endeavor to corrupt and incite you to vice; because, as you may yourself perceive, your early attainment to so great a dignity is not observed without envy, and those who could not prevent your receiving that honor will secretly endeavor to diminish it, by inducing you to forfeit the good estimation of the public; thereby precipitating you into that gulf into which they had themselves fallen; in which attempt, the consideration of your youth will give them a confidence of success. To these difficulties you ought to oppose yourself with the greater firmness, as there is at present less virtue amongst your brethren of the college. I acknowledge indeed that several of them are good and learned men, whose lives are exemplary, and whom I would recommend to you as patterns of your conduct. By emulating them you will be so much the more known and esteemed, in proportion as your age and the peculiarity of your situation will distinguish you from your colleagues. Avoid, however, as you would Scylla or Charybdis, the imputation of hypocrisy; guard against all ostentation, either in your conduct or your discourse; affect not austerity, nor ever appear too serious. This advice you will, I hope, in time understand and practice better than I can express it.

Yet you are not unacquainted with the great importance of the character which you have to sustain, for you well know that all the Christian world would prosper if the cardinals were what they ought to be; because in such a case there would always be a good pope, upon which the tranquility of Christendom so materially depends. Endeavor then to render yourself such, that if all the rest resembled you, we might expect this universal blessing. To give you particular directions as to your behavior and conversation would be a matter of no small difficulty. I shall, therefore, only recommend, that in your intercourse with the cardinals and other men of rank, your language be unassuming and respectful, guiding yourself, however, by your own reason, and not submitting to be impelled by the passions of others, who, actuated by improper motives, may pervert the use of their reasons. Let it satisfy your conscience that your conversation is without intentional offense; and if, through impetuosity of temper, any one should be offended, as his enmity is without just cause, so it will not be very lasting. On this your first visit to Rome, it will, however, be more advisable for you to listen to others than to speak much yourself.

You are now devoted to God and the church: on which account you ought to aim at being a good ecclesiastic, and to show that you prefer the honor and state of the church and of the apostolic see to every other consideration. Nor, while you keep this in view, will it be difficult for you to favor your family and your native place. On the contrary, you should be the link to bind this city closer to the church, and our family with the city; and although it be impossible to foresee what accidents may happen, yet I doubt not but this may be done with equal advantage to all: observing, however, that you are always to prefer the interests of the church.

You are not only the youngest cardinal in the college, but the youngest person that ever was raised to that rank; and you ought, therefore, to be the most vigilant and unassuming, not giving others occasion to wait for you, either in the chapel, the consistory or upon deputations. You will soon get a sufficient insight into the manners of your brethren. With those of less respectable character converse not with too much intimacy, not merely on account of the circumstance in itself, but for the sake of public opinion. Converse on general topics with all. On public occasions, let your equipage and address be rather below than above mediocrity. A handsome house and a well-ordered family will be preferable to a great retinue and a splendid residence. Endeavor to live with regularity, and gradually to bring your expenses within those bounds which in a new establishment cannot perhaps be expected. Silk and jewels are not suitable for persons in your station. Your taste will be better shown in the acquisition of a few elegant remains of antiquity, or in the collecting of handsome books, and by your attendants being learned and well-bred rather than numerous. Invite others to your house oftener than you receive invitations. Practise neither too frequently. Let your own food be plain, and take sufficient exercise, for those who wear your habit are soon liable, without great caution, to contract infirmities. The station of a cardinal is not less secure than elevated; on which account those who arrive at it too frequently become negligent; conceiving their object is attained and that they can preserve it with little trouble. This idea is often injurious to the life and character of those who entertain it. Be attentive, therefore, to your conduct, and confide in others too little rather than too much.

There is one rule which I would recommend to your attention in preference to all others. Rise early in the morning. This will not only contribute to your health, but will enable you to arrange and expedite the business of the day; and as there are various duties incident to your station, such as the performance of divine service, studying, giving audience, and so forth, you will find the observance of this admonition productive of the greatest utility. Another very necessary precaution, particularly on your entrance into public life, is to deliberate every evening on what you may have to perform the following day, that you may not be unprepared for whatever may happen. With respect to your speaking in the consistory, it will be most becoming for you at present to refer the matters in debate to the judgment of his holiness alleging as a reason your own youth and inexperience. You will probably be desired to intercede for the favors of the pope on particular occasions. Be cautious, however, that you trouble him not too often; for his temper leads him to be most liberal to those who weary him least with their solicitations. This you must observe, lest you should give him offense, remembering also at times to converse with him on more agreeable topics; and if you should be obliged to request some kindness from him, let it be done with that modesty and humility which are so pleasing to his disposition. Farewell.

DOCUMENT 20

Lorenzo de'Medici as a Collector and Patron: Excerpt from Lorenzo's *Ricordi* (Memoirs)[20]

Lorenzo de'Medici was a great collector of ancient objects and small objets de vertu, like cameos and carved gems. Unlike his father and grandfather, he was not a significant patron of large paintings or substantial buildings. As a connoisseur, he was much more private, and his collections were more suitable for personal study or intimate conversation. Lorenzo had, however, exquisite taste and deep knowledge, as well as a network of agents to acquire important pieces. Some of his collection is visible today in Florence in the Museo degli Argenti in the Palazzo Pitti.

In September of 1471 I was elected ambassador to Rome for the coronation of Pope Sixtus IV, where I was very honored, and from there I carried away two ancient marble heads with the images of Augustus and Agrippa, which the said Pope gave me; and, in addition, I took away our dish of carved chalcedony [the *Tazza Farnese*] along with many other cameos [i.e., gems] and coins which were then bought, among them the chalcedony [the *Diomedes and the Palladium*].

Excerpt from a letter of 1490 from Lorenzo to Galeotto Malatesta, thanking him for a gift of maiolica

Two days ago I received along with a letter from your Lordship those clay vases you deigned to send. [. . .] I esteem them more than if they were of silver, being very excellent and rare, as I say, and quite novel to us here. Therefore I thank Your Lordship very much, and I assure you it was not necessary to put your coat of arms on these vases to make my remembrance and recollection of your Lordship more lasting.

---

20. From Laurie Fusco and Gino Corti, *Lorenzo de'Medici: Collector and Antiquarian* (Cambridge, UK: Cambridge University Press, 2006), 6, 79, 131.

Fra Giovanni Giocondo dedicated his Corpus of Inscriptions to Lorenzo in 1489

I applied my mind to doing things that could be accomplished by time, wit and energy alone without charge or expense, and things that might interest princely minds. [. . .] If those devoted to literature take any pleasure from this [book], they should know that the credit belongs not to me but to you, who incited me in your letters to write it with the help of Alessandro Cortesi, who is most devoted to you. So it is right and just that I dedicate the work, such as it is, to your name as you are the one who shows the greatest devotion to classical antiquity.

DOCUMENT 21

The Religious Culture in Florence before Savonarola[21]

Antoninus (Antonio Pierozzi) of Florence (1389–1459) was a Dominican friar who served as prior of San Marco and archbishop of Florence from 1446 to 1459. He was widely loved and respected for his austere life and great learning, and was canonized as a saint in 1523. His Summa Theologica, *completed shortly before his death, was one of the most popular Renaissance manuals for priests and confessors, and reflects the official confessional beliefs in Florence under the Medici. It was a vast work, covering a huge range of topics, especially in moral theology. Preachers, including Savonarola, would have consulted it for source material when composing sermons. The following passage comes from a chapter praising poverty.*

On the Counsel of Poverty

Concerning poverty, which is also placed among the counsels of the Lord, there is an error made by some people: for some commend it in such a way that, as they assert, it is not licit for anyone, even a layman, to have any possession of his own, but rather it is worthy of damnation. These are called the apostolic heretics. [...] Notwithstanding what the Lord says in Luke 13, "Unless someone renounces all the things he possesses, he cannot be my disciple." For "a disciple of Christ" can be understood in two ways: one way broadly, meaning one who observes the commandments of Christ, like Nicodemus, Joseph, etc., and for these people it was appropriate to renounce all worldly things in the mind, namely in such a way that they put nothing before God and the observation of his commandments; the second way properly and strictly, meaning the state of perfection and observance of the counsels which the apostles abiding with Christ had, and for them it is appropriate to renounce love [of worldly things] and its effect, so that they should have nothing of their own in particular, as

---

21. Antonio Pierozzi (Saint Antoninus of Florence), *Summa Theologica* (Verona: Ex Typographia Seminarii, Apud Augustinum Carattonium, 1740), IV.12.3, "De consilio paupertatis." Translation by Kirsty Schut.

is the state of religious [i.e., monks]. [. . .] And Christ was speaking properly of the latter. For some so commend poverty that they say that the perfection of the rational creature consists in it. But St. Thomas [Aquinas] disproves this in the *Secunda Secundae*. [. . .]

On the other hand, some so detest poverty that they reject every level of poverty and renunciation of worldly goods, and call it illicit. But St. Thomas also disproves this in the *Summa Contra Gentiles*. [. . .]

It is good for some people to have riches, namely those who use them for virtues; for some people it is bad to have them, namely those who are drawn away from virtue by them, or by excessive care or affection for them, or by the exaltation of the mind connected with them. But there are virtues both of the active life and the contemplative life, and both need riches. For the contemplative virtues need them for the sustenance of life, and the active virtues need them both for this and in order to help others with whom one should live. For this reason, the contemplative life is also more perfect, because it needs fewer things. Indeed, it seems to pertain to this life that man is totally free to attend to divine things. Indeed, a minimum of worldly riches suffices for those pursuing this perfection, namely as much as is necessary for sustaining natural life. [. . .] Poverty is therefore laudable insofar as it liberates man from those vices in which others are implicated through riches; however, insofar as it removes the care which arises from riches, it is useful for some, namely those who are so disposed that they would be occupied in better things, but not for novices who, liberated from this care, fall into worse occupations. [. . .] But insofar as poverty impedes the good which comes from riches, namely the sustenance of oneself and the assistance of others, it is simply evil. For it is evil insofar as the assistance with which one assists one's neighbors can be made up for by a greater good, namely that a man lacking riches can more freely devote himself to divine and spiritual things. But the good of one's own sustenance is necessary to the extent that nothing else can compensate for it. For a man ought not to give up his life in the attainment of some good. Poverty therefore is very laudable when a man freed from worldly concerns devotes himself more freely to divine and spiritual things, so that while the faculty of a man remains with him, he sustains himself in a licit manner, for which not many things are required. And it is laudable to the extent that the way of living in poverty causes less care, not to the extent that the poverty is greater. For poverty is not good in itself, but insofar as it liberates one from those things by which man is impeded in such a way that he exerts himself less for spiritual goods.

For this reason, the measure of its goodness is the way in which man is liberated from the aforesaid impediments. And this is common to all external goods, which are good to the extent that they effect virtue, but not in themselves.

§1. There is a fourfold way of pursuing poverty, according to St. Thomas [Aquinas] [in the *Summa Contra Gentiles*, ch. 132]. And the first way is in such a way that, for the price of the sale of their possessions, a group of people can live communally in a college or brotherhood, but not for a long time. And therefore the Apostles set up this way of living for the faithful in Jerusalem, because they foresaw through the Holy Spirit that they would not remain long in Jerusalem, first because of the persecutions and injuries inflicted by the Jews, then because of the present destruction of the city and people, for which reason it was only necessary to provide for a short time. And because of this, they are not read to have instituted this way of living when they went over to the Gentiles, among whom the Church was to be instituted and preserved. And if it is said that fraud and theft can be committed by treasurers [*dispensatores*] in this way of living, for which reason it does not seem to be an appropriate way of living, it is responded that this is common to all modes of living in which people live together, but in this there is less, since it seems less likely that those choosing the life of perfection should commit fraud. A remedy for this is also employed in the provident management of the faithful, for which reason Stephen and the others were chosen by the apostles, because they were reputed to be fit for this office.

There is a second way of living in voluntary poverty, namely for those having possessions to live off them in common and provide for individuals as their work requires, as is observed in very many monasteries, and in just about all monks, and this is also an appropriate and laudable way. Nor through this is anything lost of the perfection to which those taking on voluntary poverty tend. For it can be done through the care of almost one or a few that possessions be procured in an appropriate way, and so others, remaining free from any care for worldly things, can devote themselves freely to spiritual things, which is the fruit of voluntary poverty. And nor is anything of the perfection of life lost for those who take on this care for others, for what they seem to have lost in the absence of calm, they recuperate in the service of charity, in which the perfection of life also consists. And nor through this manner of living is the peace removed by the fact of having goods in common; for the people who sought to assume voluntary poverty are those who condemn worldly things, and they cannot disagree over worldly goods held in common, especially because they can expect nothing of worldly goods beyond the necessities of life, and since the treasurers [*dispensatores*] should be faithful. [. . .]

The third way of living for those pursuing voluntary poverty is that they live by the work of their hands, which was the way of living that the Apostle Paul followed, and he disseminated it to others following his example and teaching. [. . .] Therefore this way is also appropriate and good. Nor is it vain, as some object, to give up worldly goods in order that they might be acquired again by the work of one's hands, since the possession of riches also requires care in procuring them, or at least in keeping them, and man's love is drawn to himself, which doesn't happen when one seeks to acquire daily sustenance through the work of one's hands in service. Moreover, a short amount of time suffices for acquiring sustenance sufficient for the necessities of life through the work of one's hands, and a small amount of care is necessary, but it is necessary to set aside a lot of time and expend a lot of care in gathering riches or a surplus of provisions through the work of one's hands, like secular craftsmen do. Nor is it contrary that the Lord says "Do not worry" [Mt. 6.31]. For he did not prohibit manual labor, but anxious mental concern for the necessities of life, working, and doing other things, which is in itself as if man doubts that he will have these things that are needed for him to live. For if divine providence sustains birds, who cannot work in those labors with which men acquire the necessities of life, those birds are also of an inferior condition; he will provide much more for men.

Also, nor can this way of living be rejected on account of the fact that this is not sufficient for some people, such as the sick and weak, who are not able to work enough to supply the necessary provisions for themselves. For neither should other rules be rejected on account of a defect which occurs in lesser people. For this also happens in natural things, and in voluntary rules. Nor is there any way of living through which it can be so provided for a man that he cannot lose something sometimes, for even riches can sometimes also be taken away through theft and robbery. Yet there remains some remedy concerning the aforesaid way of living, namely, that for one whose manual labor does not suffice for his own necessities, he will be helped by someone else from the same group, who is able to work more than is necessary for himself, or by others who possess riches, according to the law of charity and natural friendship, by which one person helps another. And it is not a problem if it is said that such people would need to spend a lot of time working and consequently would be able to spend only a little time on spiritual things. For a few things suffice for the necessities of life, and these sorts of people should be content with a few things, for which reason they would not be much impeded from spiritual works, since they would not have to expend much time on manual labor, since even while working they could think of God and praise God and do other things of this sort. They can also be helped by the assistance of others. And although manual labor is useful for avoiding idleness and subduing the flesh, voluntary poverty is not taken on for the sake of these things, since the flesh can be tamed and idleness can also be avoided in other ways.

There is also a fourth mode of poverty, namely such that those pursuing voluntary poverty, putting aside all their goods, live off those things which are given to them by others as alms, not having such possessions or revenues in common as would be sufficient to provide for themselves. And the Lord seems to have observed this mode of living with his disciples, for it is said in Luke 8 that some women followed him ministering to him from their resources. And this is the best, for nor is it inappropriate, as some object, that someone be sustained who gives up for the sake of something else something that might be useful for others, out of these things which were given by others. For unless this were the case, human society could not endure. For if everyone only took care of his own concerns, there would not be anyone who looked after the good of the community. Therefore it is best for human society that those who serve the common good, having put aside their own cares, be sustained by those whose utility they serve. For this reason, knights live off the stipends of others, and the governors of the republic are provided for from the common [purse]. However, those who take on voluntary poverty in order to follow Christ certainly put aside all things in order to serve the common good, teaching the people by example and wise instruction, and sustaining them with prayers and interventions. From which it is also apparent that they do not live wickedly off these things that are given to them by others, from which they may be compensated more heavily, accepting worldly things for sustenance and accomplishing spiritual things for others. For while they inspire others to the virtues by their examples, it happens that those for the sake of whom they are performing spiritual deeds come to love worldly things less by their example, and so are more inspired to give to them. And nor will they lose through this the freedom to admonish and condemn these people, since the things they receive are few, and since they have contempt for worldly things, so they will not be moved to leave off the salvation of their neighbors on account of the alms they have received. And nor is it inappropriate that they expose their needs in begging for themselves or for others. For even the Apostles are said to have done this for the sake of the poor who were in Jerusalem. And nor does this begging render these men contemptible, if it is done in moderation, for the sake of necessities, and not to excess, and relentlessly, without considering the condition of the people they are asking, and the time and place, which must be observed by those who pursue perfection of life. From which it follows that this begging does not have any sort of shame, which it would have if it were done with importunity and indifference, for the sake of pleasure or excess. And although begging is done as a sort of humbling, since it is necessary to beg in order to pursue the perfection of poor life, this humbling is generally of humility. For to take on a humbling is virtuous, even if our office does not require this, in order that we might inspire others by our example, for whom it will happen that they can bear it more easily, and sometimes we use mortifications for the sake of virtue, as a sort of medicine, for instance: when someone's soul is prone to immoderate superiority, after having observed appropriate moderation, one uses mortifications imposed voluntarily or by someone else to suppress the elevation of the soul.

DOCUMENT 22

The Expulsion of the Medici as Described by the Diarist Luca Landucci[22]

Luca Landucci (1436–1516, see above p. 101), the Florentine apothecary and diarist, described in a day-by-day commentary the events that led to the expulsion of Piero di Lorenzo de'Medici and his brothers. He was an eyewitness to these dramatic events and so provides a vivid narrative of the end of the Medici hegemony in November 1494.

9th November (Sunday). About 20 in the afternoon (4 p.m.), when it was ringing for vespers, Piero son of Lorenzo de' Medici wished to go to the *Signoria* in the *Palagio* [Palazzo della Signoria], taking his armed men with him. The *Signoria* not allowing this, he did not choose to go alone, and turned back. Now men began to collect in the Piazza, and in the *Palagio* were heard cries of *Popolo e Libertà!* (The People and Liberty!), whilst the bell was rung for a *parlamento*, and men appeared at the windows with the same cry. Immediately the *Gonfaloniere del Bue* [the standardbearer of the Ox Quarter of Florence, that is, around Santa Croce] came into the Piazza, and behind him Francesco Valori and other citizens on horseback, all crying *Popolo e Libertà!* These were the first to arrive; but before an hour had passed, the Piazza was filled with all the *Gonfaloni* and all the citizens, troops of armed men crying loudly, *Popolo e Libertà!* Although the people did not very well understand what all this tumult was about, nevertheless not many citizens went to Piero de' Medici's house. The Tornabuoni and some other citizens went there armed, with many men under their command, and coming into the street before his door, cried, *Palle!* Piero then mounted his horse, to come into the Piazza with his men, starting several times, and then stopping again. I think that he perceived how few citizens were with him, and also he must have been told that the Piazza was full of armed men. Meanwhile the cardinal, his brother, left his house, accompanied by many soldiers and by those citizens who were there, and came down the *Corso* as far as

22. From Luca Landucci, *A Florentine Diary*, 60–72.

Orto San Michele [Orsanmichele], crying *Popolo e Libertà!* like the rest; declaring that he separated himself from Piero. The only consequence was that the Piazza turned against him, menacing him with the points of their weapons, shouting at him as a traitor, and not choosing to accept him. He turned back, not without danger. And now a proclamation was issued, at the *Canto della Macina* and in the *Via de' Martegli* next to the *Chiassolino* [little alley], ordering every foreigner to lay down his arms, and forbidding anyone on pain of death to aid or abet Piero de' Medici. In consequence of this, many abandoned Piero and laid down their arms. They dropped off on all sides, so that few remained with him. Therefore Piero left his house and went towards the *Porta a San Gallo*, which he had caused to be kept open for him by his brother Giuliano with many soldiers and by friends outside. Signor Pagolo Orsini was waiting outside with horses and armed men in readiness to enter, but it did not seem the right moment, and when Piero arrived they decided it would be best to go away, taking Giuliano with them. The poor young cardinal remained in his house, and I saw him at a window kneeling with joined hands, praying Heaven to have mercy. I was much touched when I saw him, considering him to be a good lad and of upright character. It was said that when he had seen Piero ride away, he disguised himself as a monk and took his departure also. Another proclamation was published in the Piazza, announcing that whoever slew Piero de' Medici should have 2 thousand ducats and whoever slew the cardinal should have a thousand. And after this many soldiers left the Piazza with Jacopo de' Nerli, and going to the house of Ser Giovanni son of Ser Bartolomeo, pillaged it. And then the crowd rose, with the cry of *Antonio di Bernardo*, and pillaged his house also, and pillaged the Bargello. The number of soldiers and of the people going about robbing increased every moment; and this all happened before 24 in the evening (8 p.m.), less than four hours from when the disturbance began. Then the *Signoria* published a proclamation forbidding any more houses to be pillaged, on pain of death; and the *Gonfaloni* went about the city all night to guard it, crying *Popolo e Libertà!*, carrying lighted torches, so that no more harm was done, except that a certain serving-man of the *Bargello* who cried *Palle*, was killed in the Piazza. And now Girolamo, son of Marabotto Tornabuoni, and Pierantonio Carnesecchi, and others of that party, turned and cried *Popolo e Libertà!* like the rest. When they were about to enter the Piazza, however, weapons were pointed against them, and they were only saved by their cuirasses, and had to escape as best they might. In fact, Girolamo Tornabuoni had his cuirass torn off in Orto San Michele, but when he begged for mercy, his life was spared. And Giovan Francesco Tornabuoni was severely wounded in the throat, and returned home. When the disturbance began, some of the French who were quartered in Florence armed themselves and joined Piero's party, crying *Francia* [France]. I believe that it was pointed out to them that the matter was between citizens only, and that if they were to do anything against the *Palagio* [Palazzo della Signoria, seat of the Priors], they would put themselves in the wrong; therefore they acted accordingly, returning to their lodgings and then going about the city unarmed.

10th November (Monday). The citizens again came armed into the Piazza, and sent to recruit more men. Antonio di Bernardo, Ser Giovanni son of Ser Bartolomeo, Ser Simone da Staggia, Ser Ceccone son of Ser Barone, Ser Lorenzo of the Dogana, Lorenzo son of Giovanni Tornabuoni, and Piero Tornabuoni, were fetched from their houses and made prisoner. The Signoria published a proclamation commanding anyone who either had, or knew of anyone who had, property belonging to Piero de' Medici or to the cardinal his brother, or to Ser Giovanni, Ser Simone, Ser Bernardo, and Ser Lorenzo of the Dogana, to declare it, on pain of death. And a second proclamation was published, which had been decided upon by the council composed of all the *veduti e seduti* [those citizens who were eligible for office]. There were an immense number of citizens present. And this morning they pillaged the cardinal's house, which was in Sant'Antonio di Firenze, sending their men to claim the last things that still remained.

11th November (Tuesday). A man arrived in the Piazza, having entered the city by the *Porta alla Croce*, and said that he had passed men-at-arms and infantry on the road to Florence, belonging to Piero de' Medici. Cries of *Popolo e Libertà* immediately resounded everywhere, and in less than half an hour the whole city was in arms, men of all classes rushing to the Piazza with incredible haste, and with deafening cries of *Popolo e Libertà*. I verily believe that if the whole world had come against them, such a union could not have been broken; it being permitted by the Lord that the people should make such a demonstration, during this danger from the French, who had come to Florence with the evil intent of sacking it. But when they saw of what sort the people were, their heart failed them. As soon as the truth was known, that no armed men were approaching, a proclamation was made ordering all to lay aside their weapons, and this was about the dinner-hour. The *Gonfaloni*, however, remained on guard day and night, with a good number of men; and horsemen and foot-soldiers belonging to the King of France were continually entering. The *Signoria* had had the *Porta di San Friano* [Frediano] opened. This evening the King of France remained at Empoli; and more than 6 thousand men came before the king, and as many with him, and another 6 thousand behind him. And at this time the taxes were lightened and many pardons granted.

12th November (Wednesday). Lorenzo son of Piero Francesco de' Medici returned, and dined at his own house of the Gora, and the same evening he went to meet the king, who was stopping at Legniaia, in the house of Piero Capponi. And on this same day the *Bargello* was made prisoner in the church of the *Servi*. Also more French entered the city than any other day, and they filled every house, even the poorest, including all Camaldoli.

13th November (Thursday). We heard that the Pisans had risen and taken possession of the city; and pulling down a certain marble *marzocco* [lion, a symbol of Florence], had dragged it all over Pisa, and then thrown it into the Arno, crying, "*Libertà!*" We also heard that Piero and his brothers were at Bologna; and such a crowd of French and Swiss were coming into Florence that there was great confusion and alarm and suspicion amongst all classes. You may think what it was to have all this crowd in our houses, and everything left as usual, with the women about, and to have to serve them with whatever they needed, at the greatest inconvenience.

14th November (Friday). Lorenzo, son of Francesco de' Medici, and his brother, and several other exiled citizens, returned to Florence, because the sentences were remitted of all those who had been exiled from 1434 onwards. Observe that Lorenzo de' Medici and his brother were also reinstated in their rights. And every house in the city was full.

15th November (Saturday). Numbers of French were still coming in; and preparations were made to receive the king with great honour.

16th November (Sunday). Many decorations were made for the king's arrival in the house of Piero de' Medici, and principally at the entrance of the palace. Two large columns were erected outside, one on each side of the gate, with ornamentation representing the arms of France, etc., too intricate to describe. It truly was a triumph; everything was done so well and on such a grand scale. I will not even begin to tell you how the interior was ordered. And *spiritegli* and giants and triumphal cars went about the town, and stages on wheels for the miracle-play of the *Nunziata*, whilst there were innumerable embellishments and the arms of France all over Florence. Above the gate of the Palagio de' Signori were the said arms, very large and magnificently blazoned.

17th November. The King of France entered Florence at 22 in the evening (6 p.m.) by the Porta a San Friano, and passed through the Piazza (de' Signori), proceeding so slowly that it was already 24 (8 p.m.) before he reached Santa Maria del Fiore. He dismounted at the steps, and walked up to the High Altar, there being so many torches that they made a double row from the door to the altar, leaving a way clear in the middle, along which he went with his barons and all his suite, amidst such tumultuous shouting of *Viva Francia* as was never heard. Only think that all Florence was there, either in the church or outside. Everyone shouted, great and small, old and young, and all from their hearts, without flattery. When he was seen on foot he seemed to the people somewhat less imposing, for he was in fact a very small man. Nevertheless there was no one who did not feel favourably disposed towards him. Therefore it should have been easy to make him understand that our hearts are innocent of guile, and that we are truly devoted to him; so that he ought to feel moved towards us in uncommon measure, and to trust us absolutely. This is really the case, and he will see in the future what the faith of the Florentines signifies. Upon coming out of church, he remounted his horse and rode on to the palace of Piero de' Medici, amidst continued cries of *Viva Francia*. Never was such joy seen before, or so much honour done to anyone, with heartfelt sincerity, as we were in hopes that he would bring us peace and rest. In the end it proved not to be so, as he took Pisa from us and gave it to the Pisans, which he had no right to do, seeing that he could not give what was not his.

18th November (Tuesday). The said king went to hear mass in San Lorenzo, and I was at the same mass, and saw him quite close.

19th November. He again heard mass in San Lorenzo; and then went for a ride through Florence, going to see the lions. And it was his wish that some of the prisoners in the Palagio del Capitano [Palace of the Captain of the People, i.e., the Bargello] should be liberated, those namely who were detained for political reasons; amongst them a Ser Lorenzo, and an Andrea, and others; and this desire of his to benefit the prisoners on the occasion of his passing through the town was granted.

20th November (Thursday). There were murmurs all over the city to the effect that the king wished to reinstate Piero de' Medici, and the ruling citizens seemed much vexed about this matter.

21st November (Friday). About 21 in the evening (5 p.m.) the *Signori* called a council of the most worthy men in the city, and explained to them how the king had said one thing and now wished another, and how he

demanded the reinstatement of Piero de' Medici, and asked them what
answer they advised to be given him. And they all replied to the effect that
Piero's return could not be consented to upon any condition whatever,
even if the king wished it; and that the king should be told that everything else but this would be granted him. They declared, moreover, that
if it were necessary to take up arms, they should go against the king and
everyone who differed from them saying, "If the king has 20 thousand
men, we can call up 50 thousand of our own in the city"; showing no fear
of the king, and also showing that a great hatred had arisen between the
citizens and this Piero de' Medici; why this was, the Lord alone knows.
At this time, as it pleased God, there was a little disturbance in the *Piazza
de' Signori*, all the people being suspicious, and excited at the least noise,
and always on the look-out for some danger. They really lived in dread
and a sort of dismay, mostly caused by having their houses full of the
French. And it was continually being repeated that the king had promised his soldiers Florence should be sacked. Therefore, as soon as there
was this little disturbance in the Piazza, everyone hastened home, and all
the shops were closed, one sending his silk goods and another his woollen
goods away to his house or to some place of security. This suspicion was
tacit, not a word being said; but many of the French, no less dismayed
than we were, suspecting they knew not what, took up arms, and seized
the *Porta a San Friano* and the bridges, so as to be able to escape. Possibly
it had been so arranged among themselves beforehand, in case it should
be needful. The result was that the *Signoria* and the council who had held
the aforesaid consultation, when they heard that all the shops were being
closed, felt still more acutely the danger of Piero's return; and the Signori
urged the most worthy men of the council to go to the king and point out
to him the danger of the city, begging him not to demand this thing, as
it could only entail evil, etc. Hence the king, seeing the opposition of the
citizens, and also realising his own danger, replied:"I am not here to cause
disturbances, but to bring peace; and if I thought of this thing, it was only
in the idea of pleasing the people and everyone. I wish for nothing but the
general good, and no more need be said about Piero's return." Then the
citizens made this offer to the king:"Whatever you may be pleased to ask
from us freely, we shall be ready to bring to your aid." Thereupon the king
asked that the city of Florence should lend him 120 thousand florins, 50
thousand to be paid at once, and 70 thousand before the end of July; and
besides this, that for the duration of the war they should lend him 12
thousand a year. After the end of the war, our city should be left entirely

free; and whether he died, or whether he conquered or not, it should still be left free. He only demanded the forts of Pisa and a few others that he had taken, Sarzana, etc., so that he should be able to return in safety to his country. He did not receive a reply immediately. Everyone said that a little time was needed, on account of the money.

22nd November (Saturday). The city was in great dread of being pillaged, and it was considered a bad sign that the king did not wish to sign the agreement. The French seemed to be becoming more and more masters of the place; they did not allow the citizens to go about armed, day or night, but took away their weapons, and kept striking and stabbing them. No one ventured to speak or to go out after the Ave Maria (at 5 o'clock); and the French went about robbing in the night, their guards parading the city. Everyone was so discouraged and intimidated that when they saw anyone carrying stones or gravel they went crazy and struck out.

23rd November (Sunday). The king rode out with a great troop of horsemen, and came to the *Croce di San Giovanni*; and when he was near the steps of Santa Maria del Fiore, he turned back and went towards the *Servi* [Servite Church]; but having gone a few paces, he turned round again, and again went to the *Croce di San Giovanni*, going at the back of *San Giovanni*, through that narrow *Chiassolino*, and coming under the *Volta di San Giovanni, d'Cialdonai*; and those who saw him laughed, and said slighting things of him, causing his reputation to suffer. Then he went through the *Mercato Vecchio*, and on as far as *San Felice in Piazza*, to see the *festa* of San Felice, which they were having on his account; but when he reached the door he would not enter; and they repeated everything several times, but he did not enter once. Many people said that he was afraid, and did not wish to be shut in, and this proved to us that he was more afraid than we were; and woe to him if a disturbance had begun, although there would also have been great danger for us. But the Lord has always helped us, on account of the prayers of His servants and of the number of holy monks and nuns in the city, who are in truth on their way to God. At this time two Venetian ambassadors to the king arrived, and there were also the Genoese ambassadors, who came, it was said, to demand Serezzana and other things from him.

24th November (Monday). There was much whispering amongst the people, who said suspiciously: "This king doesn't know what he wishes; he has not yet signed the agreement." And many declared that some of his counsellors were endeavouring to hinder it, as there was a certain Signore di Bre, lodging in the house of Giovanni Tornabuoni, who said that he had promised some people to get Piero reinstated, and to persuade the king to ask for this, but perhaps it was not true. This was, as I say, the opinion of many of the citizens, and therefore they were in great dread; still more so when it was said that the king was going this morning to dine in the *Palagio* with the *Signoria*, and that he had caused all the armed men to be removed from the *Palagio*, and he was going there with many armed men, so that everyone suspected him of evil designs. There was no one who did not take pains this morning to fill his house with bread and with weapons and with stones, and to strengthen his house as much as possible, everyone being of the mind and intention to die fighting, and to slay anyone if needful, in the manner of the Sicilian Vespers. And fear was so widespread that when at the dinner hour people began to say *Serra, serra!* (Shut everything!), it came about that the whole of Florence locked itself in, one fleeing here and another there, without any fresh cause or disturbance, the consequence being that many of the French rushed to the *Porta a San Friano* and took possession of the *Ponte alla Carraia*. And in *Borgo Ognissanti* and in *Via Palazzuolo*, and in *Borgo San Friano*, so many stones were thrown from the windows that they were not able to get to the gates; and when they asked the reason of it, no one knew. Therefore the king did not go to dine in the *Palagio*; and, by divine permission, the French became so uneasy that it caused them to change their evil intentions towards us who only had good ones. Anyone can see that God does not abandon Florence, but we are not sufficiently grateful. At this time we heard that the French troops which had been in Romagna were passing by in the neighbourhood of Dicomano.

25th November (Tuesday). There was nothing new, except that the French were so alarmed that they stood on guard night and day. They took the citizens' arms from them, and robbed anyone whom they encountered at night; so that some of those bold Florentines who had had the idea of slaying the French when they met them at night, were themselves slain or wounded. If the French had stayed longer they (these rash Florentines) would have gone the right way to work to bring about trouble. It is always the case that certain thoughtless men endanger cities, not considering what it means to kindle the spark; it may happen that a man of no account arouses the anger of a king by some piece of folly, without the city being to blame.

26th November (Wednesday). The king went together with the *Signoria* to hear mass at *Santa Maria del Fiore*, and here he swore to observe the articles which had been drawn up, and which were as follows: that we should lend him 120 thousand florins, giving him 50 thousand florins now, and the rest before the end of July 1495; and that he should leave and give back to us the forts of Pisa and all the others; and leave our territory free and unmolested; and that Piero de' Medici should be confined to boundaries 100 miles away from Florence; and that the price of 2000 florins placed upon his head should be taken off, and also off his brothers'. All this he swore to observe, on the altar of *Santa Maria del Fiore*, before Christ Jesus, on the word of a king.

27th November (Thursday). The king went out to see certain tents which had been set up on the *Prato d'Ognissanti*, and which had been presented to him by the Duke of Ferrara; there being one for the king himself that was really magnificent, with a sitting-room, a bedroom, and a chapel, and many other things besides. He was to have left this morning, but did not do so; the joy-bells were rung and bonfires were made. This morning more of the troops from Romagna reached Dicomano, and were quartered there, about 20 horses being put into my place even. I left my young son Benedetto there, and they nearly slew him several times, although he paid them proper respect, as I had impressed upon him. It was at a great cost to us. They were quartered everywhere, in the *Val di Sieve*, as far as the *Ponte a Sieve* and the *Sieci*, and then they went on along the upper valley of the Arno.

28th November (Friday). The king left Florence after having dined, and went for the night to the *Certosa*, and all his men went before or after him, so that few remained here. It was said that Fra Girolamo of Ferrara [Savonarola], our famous preacher, had gone to the king and declared that he was not doing the will of God in stopping, and that he ought to leave. It was even said that he went a second time, when he saw that the king did not leave, and declared again that he was not following God's will, and that whatever evil should befall others would return on his head. It was thought that this was the cause of his leaving more speedily, because at that time the said Fra Girolamo was held to be a prophet and a man of holy life, both in Florence and throughout Italy. At the same time there came to Florence the captain of the French troops in Romagna, whose name was Begni, and he told the king rather dictatorially that he ought to leave on every account, as the weather was favourable, and he declared that it would be ill to delay the advance. And in fact the king did leave, for he put more faith in this seigneur than in all the rest, and deservedly, as he was an extremely intelligent and worthy man, according to what was said; and this was in reality the strongest reason which induced him to leave.

DOCUMENT 23

Savonarola's *Treatise on Florentine Government*[23]

Savonarola's Treatise on Florentine Government *was likely written in the first months of 1498. In this treatise, Savonarola lays out his vision for Florentine republican institutions.*

Book 1, ch. 3:
Civil government is the most appropriate
for the city of Florence

There can be no doubt, if one pays close attention to what I have said, that if the Florentine people were to tolerate the rule of a single monarch, this man would be a wise, just, and good prince, not a tyrant. Once we examine the opinions and the ideas of erudite philosophers and theologians, however, we shall see that the Florentines, because of their nature, are not suited for this form of government. The rule of a prince—they argue—is fitting for people who are servile by nature, lacking in either courage or intelligence or both. A people that lacks intelligence, despite being physically strong, sanguine, and valorous in war, can easily be ruled by a prince. Owing to their weak intellect, such people are unable to plot against the prince, and they follow him as bees follow their queen, as we can see in people from the north. Peoples like those of the Orient, by contrast, who possess a sharp and quick intellect but lack valor, are easily conquered and live quietly under the authority of a prince. Such a situation occurs even more frequently when a people lacks both courage and intelligence. Only a tyrant, however, can impose complete rule on intelligent, bold, and courageous peoples. By virtue of their intelligence, these people continually plot against their prince and carry out their conspiracies thanks to their audacity. The Italians are such a people, whose past and present history shows that the rule of a prince never lasts. We see that despite its small size, Italy is ruled by as many princes as there are cities, and the latter never live in peace.

---

23. From Girolamo Savonarola, selections from *A Treatise on Florentine Government* in *Images of Quattrocento Florence*, 252–65.

Among the Italians, history demonstrates that the Florentines make best use of their resourceful intelligence and are bold in spirit. Although the Florentines may seem meek and exclusively devoted to their mercantile activities, they are incredibly bellicose when engaged in either a war with foreigners or civil war. Their chronicles of wars fought against powerful princes and tyrants, to whom they have never surrendered, show how they manage to defend themselves, fight, and win. The nature of this people is such that it cannot tolerate the rule of a prince, even if he be a good and perfect ruler. Evil citizens, often astute and courageous, and always more numerous and more ambitious than good citizens, try either to kill or to overthrow a prince. Princes, in turn, would have to become tyrants in order to defend their own authority. If we carefully consider the Florentine people, however, we shall see that their customs—which are as important as their character—make them unsuited not only for the rule of a prince but also for that of an aristocracy. Just as nature provides beings and objects with certain immutable predispositions—like a rock that falls and can only rise thanks to an external force—habits and customs can become natural inclinations. Even evil customs are difficult to eradicate from individuals and from a people as a whole once they have become part of their nature.

The Florentines have been accustomed to civil government for a long time, so much so that this form of rule, besides suiting their nature better than any other, is also so deeply rooted in their spirit and their habits that it is difficult or nearly impossible to change them. Even the tyrants who have come to rule in Florence as of late have not attempted to wield their power in blatant ways. They have governed wisely, not forcing the Florentines to betray their nature and give up their traditions. These tyrants have preserved the city's institutions and offices, seeing to it, however, that only their friends obtained posts in the government. The structure of civil government has therefore remained intact; this is why trying to change or replace such a deeply rooted system would mean forcing the people into something against their nature. Such an attempt would probably cause immense confusion and dissent in the community, not to mention a complete loss of freedom, as history, the teacher of every art, has shown. Whenever power has come into the hands of [a few] distinguished Florentines, the community has immediately suffered from bitter discord, and they have not found peace until one faction has driven the other out and someone has become a tyrant. The sole ruler, then, has always outraged the Florentines by depriving them of their freedom and well-being by rousing them to discontent and restlessness. If the city of Florence was once divided and filled with internal dissension because of the ambition and the enmity of the leading citizens, it would be even more so today, were it not for the grace and mercy of God. It is thanks to Him that those who have been exiled by the rulers, especially since 1434, have returned to their home city. During these last years, moreover, many a hatred has been smoldering in the city on account of the wrongs committed by certain families. Had God not intervened, such hatred would have caused much bloodshed, the destruction of many families, and various struggles and civil wars within and outside the city walls. The events that recently took place upon the arrival of the king of France should have signalled the ruin of Florence to any intelligent person who witnessed them. The council and the civil government—established by God and not by men—have been the instruments of divine will by which the city through the words of its noble citizens, both men and women, has managed to defend and preserve its freedom. Considering the dangers Florence has encountered in the last three years, there is no one who would deem it to be governed and protected by anyone other than God Himself, except for one whose sins have made him lose his common sense entirely.

We can therefore conclude that because of the divine will, from which the present civil government derives, and because of the reasons mentioned above, civil government is the best type of rule for Florence, although in and of itself, it is not the best type of rule. A solitary rule, monarchy, is the most perfect form of rule, yet it is not ideal for the Florentine people. Likewise, although monastic rule represents spiritual perfection, it is not the best form of living, and sometimes not even good at all, for many Christians. For this people, other ways of life are more appropriate, despite the fact that these other lifestyles might not be exemplary in and of themselves.

We have thus illustrated our first point, namely, which form of government is best for Florence. Now it is time to explicate the second point: what the worst form of government is for this city.

DOCUMENT 24

The Faith of Christ Is True, Because It Causes Men to Lead a Perfect Life[24]

Savonarola wrote a treatise, The Triumph of the Cross, *in 1497 to prove his Catholic orthodoxy in the face of heresy charges within Florence and, most ominously, from Rome. Although it is in many ways a traditional statement of faith and theology, there are elements that reflect the friar's belief in the necessary connection between God's plan and the social and political order on earth, and consequently his attempt to create the New Jerusalem in Florence.*

In proving Christianity to be true, we have hitherto made use of arguments founded on the good life of true Christians. We will now proceed to examine the causes of this virtuous life. One of the chief causes is, as the Scripture teaches, the belief in Christ informed by charity: "The justice of God, by faith of Jesus Christ, unto all, and upon all them that believe in Him" (Rom. iii. 22). "Without faith it is impossible to please God" (Heb. xi. 6). By faith informed by charity, we mean that, loving Christ crucified above all things, we believe Him to be truly God and truly Man, One with the Father and the Holy Ghost, and distinct from them only in Person.

Universal experience demonstrates the truth of what we say. For in the present day it is evident to all, and still more was it so in days gone by, that, as soon as a man grasps the Faith of Christ and becomes inflamed with His love, he begins to lead a Christian life, and makes progress in perfection, in proportion to his increase of faith and charity; and at the same time he is confirmed in those virtues, in proportion to his advance in perfection. On the other hand, they who lead bad lives are deficient in faith; and they that lack faith lead bad lives. As this is a truth admitting no denial, we will investigate it, and, by inquiring into the causes of such wonderful effects, will deduce proofs of the truth of the Christian religion.

---

24. Girolamo Savonarola, *The Triumph of the Cross*, ed. and trans., with Introduction by the Very Rev. Father John Procter, S.T.L. (London: Sands & Co., 1901), 51–54.

First. Since all perfection depends upon its cause, no effect can be more perfect than its cause. Therefore, if all the truth and uprightness of the Christian life depends upon the Faith of Christ, as upon its cause, it is impossible that Christ is God, and that His religion is the true religion revealed by God Again. It is impossible that falsehood and evil should be the cause of truth and goodness; for evil, in so far as it is evil, and falsehood, in so far as it is falsehood, are nothingness. If, then, the Faith of Christ were false, His love would be vain and evil. Now, a life so perfect as is the Christian life could not spring from falsehood and iniquity. Therefore, the Christian religion must be true.

Furthermore. If this religion be untrue it is the most stupid falsehood that can possibly be conceived; for to say (were it not true) that a crucified man is God could be the extreme of folly. Now, as the Christian life is a perfect life, it cannot spring from untruth; for all rightly ordered life proceeds from correctness of understanding, and all error in human conduct springs from some mistake on the part of the intellect.

It must also be remembered that capacity for improvement in any nature is proportioned to the good disposition already existing therein. Now, as the perfection of our intellect is truth, and as purity of heart is the disposition which enables him to become steadfast in truth, the more a man is purged from earthly affections the better he will know the truth, the more closely he will embrace it, and the further he will banish falsehood from his soul. If this be true, surely Christians, since their lives are purer than those of other men, would be the first to know if their religion were false. We see, however, that far from rejecting their faith, Christians cling more closely to it in proportion as they increase in perfection, and that their increase in perfection is proportioned to their steadfastness in their faith. Therefore, their faith cannot be false.

Again, as God is the First Cause moving all things, both spiritual and corporal, it is certain that it is He who must move the human understanding, and that, apart from Him, no truth can be known. But who can doubt that God will inspire to know the truth those who are prepared for its reception, rather than those who are not thus disposed, and especially when the truth concerns eternal salvation? Since then true Christians are better prepared than are any other men to embrace the truth, we cannot doubt that, if the Faith of Christ were false, they would be enlightened by God to reject it. To think otherwise, would be to doubt the providence and goodness of God.

The end regulates the means used to attain it, and he that errs as to his end, will err also as to the means which he uses. Christians do not err as to the means which they adopt for attaining to beatitude, and therefore they do not err as to their end. Now, as all Christians profess that Christ is their End, and that they strive to be made like to Him in this life in order to enjoy Him in the next, it cannot be erroneous to teach that Christ is God, and is the End of human life.

Again, God proceeds in all things in a certain order, and in His wisdom governs inferior things by those that are superior to them. And since the cause is always more perfect than the effect, He has ordained noblest causes for the noblest effects. As there is not in the world a more noble effect than the Christian life, it follows that the cause from which it springs must be the noblest possible. Since the Christian life is an effect of the Faith of Christ, we must acknowledge that that Faith, far from being a fable, is the noble cause of a noble effect.

All secondary causes are instruments of a primary cause. Therefore Christ, the Man who was crucified, is the instrument whereby God chooses to produce that wonderful effect—the Christian life. Had Christ, in spite of His assertions, not been God, His pride and mendacity would have been unparalleled; and God would have used a bad instrument to produce a most perfect effect—a course quite out of keeping with His wisdom.

The more closely an effect resembles its cause, the more perfect does it become. We become more holy and more Divine in proportion as we walk in the footsteps of Christ and become like to Him. This is a clear proof that Christ is true God, and the Cause of man.

Causes are known by their effects, and one of the best arguments in favour of the Christian religion is the reflection that, whereas heathen philosophers have laboured for years to establish rules of conduct, they have gained but few disciples, of whom even the most virtuous have never attained to that standard of living which has been so quickly reached by innumerable Christians of both sexes and of every race and condition. No one who reflects on this fact can fail to see that there is no comparison between the efficacy of the heathen philosophy and of the Christian Faith, which is able to render the proud, avaricious, and luxurious, humble, benevolent and chaste. Every one, consequently, must acknowledge that Christ, as God, is the Principal Cause of human perfection, and, as Man, is its Means and Instrumental Cause.

DOCUMENT 25

An Anonymous Florentine Prophecy with *Fraticelli* Mystical References[25]

There was a deep mystical tradition among Italians, including Florentines. Visions and prophecies often reflected challenging times, such as war, plague, or famine; and occasionally there were clear political intentions, as in the prophecy below, which references the exceptional mission of Florence, the alliance with the French king, and the eventual coming of an age of peace and power. Many of these prophecies had roots in the preaching of the Fraticelli, *or Spiritual Franciscans, those followers of St. Francis who championed humility, poverty, and the exaltation of the oppressed. Savonarola would access this tradition and appropriate its message in his sermons and prophecies, despite Pope Boniface VIII having declared the sect heretical in 1296.*

The she-bear of tribulation rises from her den. The swords of the philosophers clash. This stands for the teachings of the ancient prophets, sages, and astrologers, for they all appear to contend with one another. In examining them properly, however, it will become clear that they all have said the same thing. The bear represents the mother of scandalous action—more precisely, the hope of those who believe they save themselves by murdering their neighbors. She will be so thoroughly annihilated that barely even the memory of her will remain.

The whorelike she-wolf licks the blood of the she-bear, leaves her husband, and commits adultery with a strange beast. This refers to the hypocritical preachers and those who do not fight against the she-bear.

The angels shudder. They are the good people, that is, the orphans and the children who live in peace.

The birds cry. They are the ones who see things from above and the diviners of ancient times.

---

25. From Florence, BNC, MS. Magl. 25.344, ff. 31–32, in *Images of Quattrocento Florence*, 236–37.

The lion rises and attacks the she-wolf, wounding her with his paws. That is, the aforementioned city [Florence] will retaliate against the she-wolf by taking all her possessions and domains.

A new bloodshed reddens the wet plain. There will be a battle between the French and the Germans in the said plain, namely in the plain of the hot springs.

The city which is the daughter of Rome has become the mistress and capital of all those around. This means Florence, originally called Romolina, and later named after Florin, the Roman king who founded her. The eagle will make her nest there, and she will become mistress of all the western cities.

She joins forces with the Gaul and fights most valiantly. That means with the royal family of France, for in ancient times the French were called Gauls.

The wicked and the kings flee. These are the treacherous lords who have been perfidious and cruel.

Weapons will be hated, and God will bring peace from heaven to the people who live on earth. The sea will open, and from it will emerge a new crown. This means that a great power will bring peace to all Christendom.

Having risen from the bed of pain where he has lain for a long time, the lion will grow stronger. Peace will flourish, and there will be harmony among the beasts in the garden. The astrologers will be silent. The latter are the treacherous and cruel lords who have murdered out of greed. A new shepherd will come from a place other than the dominion of St. Silvester, and he will be guarded by the angels. Mass will be celebrated with songs, prayers, and holy sacrifice.

DOCUMENT 26

Laude (Song) from the Early Fourteenth-Century Laudario of a Florentine Confraternity, the Company of Santo Spirito[26]

This Laude *comes from the Company of Santo Spirito, a small confraternity (an association of laymen for religious purposes). The* confratelli *celebrated in the church of Santo Spirito in Florence. Laudi such as this would likely have been sung by a soloist or a choir, with responses from the congregation.*

> *A voi, gente, facciam prego*
>
> People, we exhort you
> to be penitent;
> be afraid
> of the strong reproach
> that the high God of Heaven
> will make at the judgment
> at which all of us will be present.
>
> As the sun
> appears in the Orient,
> so will our Lord
> in truth appear;
> he will come with such splendor
> that all people will see him
> and everyone will tremble with fear.
>
> Souls will be gathered around
> from the four corners;
> at the sound of a trumpet

---

26. From *The Florence Laudario: An Edition of Florence, Biblioteca Nazionale Centrale, Banco Rari 18, Volume 2*, trans. and eds. Blake McDowell Wilson and Nello Barbieri (Madison, WI: A-R Editions, 1995), text 4, lii–liii.

they will rise again;
in the blink of an eye
all people will be there,
people from the world over.

He will appear on the throne
of majesty
to judge those
whom he had invited,
but who did not go to the banquet
when they heard the call;
he will send them to the place of sorrow.

DOCUMENT 27

Savonarola, Aggeus, Sermon 13, Delivered December 14, 1494[27]

This is from a much longer sermon delivered on the third Sunday of Advent. In it Savonarola identifies the structure of the government he thinks most appropriate for the Florentine republic and the new moral order he demanded for the city. Aggeus refers to Haggai, a Jewish prophet (c. 500 BC), who preached that the Temple of Solomon in Jerusalem should be rebuilt.

[…] Furthermore, it is necessary that the Magnificent Signory ordain that all those things contrary to godly religion be removed from the city, and in the first place, to act and ordain that the clergy must be good, because priests have to be a mirror to the people wherein everyone beholds and learns righteous living. But let the bad priests and religious be expelled; I do not say that you do it on your own—that you deprive them of their benefices—but with the authority of the Supreme Pontiff see to it that the clergy and the religious of your city are good. They should not puff themselves up with so much material wealth, but give it to the very poor for God's sake and let go their superfluities, and in this way they would gain Paradise. It is necessary, I say, to see that the clergy are good and everything is reformed.

Likewise, it is necessary that the Signory pass laws against that accursed vice of sodomy, for which you know that Florence is infamous throughout the whole of Italy; this infamy arises perhaps from your talking and chattering about it so much, so that there is not so much in deeds, perhaps, as in words. Pass a law, I say, and let it be without mercy; that is, let these people be stoned and burned. On the other hand, it is necessary that you remove from among yourselves these poems and games and

---

27. From Girolamo Savonarola, *Aggeus* [Haggai, a prophetic book of Hebrew and Christian texts], Sermon 13, December 14, 1494, in *Selected Writings of Girolamo Savonarola on Religion and Politics, 1490–1498*, ed. and trans. A. Borelli and M. Passaro (New Haven, CT: Yale University Press, 2006), 157–58.

taverns and the evil fashion of women's clothes, and, likewise, we must throw out everything that is noxious to the health of the soul. Let everyone live for God and not for the world, all in simplicity and charity, so that we may all sing: *Ecce quam bonum et quam iocundum habitare fratres in unum.* [...]

DOCUMENT 28

The Bands of Hope and the Expulsion of the Jews, 1496, from the *History of Piero Parenti*[28]

Piero Parenti (1450–1519), son of the diarist and merchant Marco Parenti, continued his father's History. *He was educated as a humanist, including a period of study with Marsilio Ficino, and had a great reputation as a Latin translator. Although he was sympathetic to Savonarola early in the Dominican's career in Florence, he soon distanced himself, as did his teacher Ficino, when Savonarola's sermons became more extravagant. He was elected as one of the Eight on Security (the Otto di Guardia), an office responsible for criminal proceedings against citizens, in April of 1498, and consequently examined Savonarola at his trials.*

Although it had been suggested before by other preachers that it would be well to expel the Jews from Florence and set up the *Monte di Pietà*, now especially this idea took fire, supported by the preacher at Santa Croce and not contradicted by Fra Girolamo. Because it was customary to have a procession and solemn celebration at the inauguration of such an undertaking, they combined the procession meant to carry out the *Monte [di Pietà]* and the children organized by Fra Girolamo for Palm Sunday, and the children, in their new habits, prayed to God to remove His anger against this land and to free us from plague and from all other imminent adversities. Their habit was such that on top of their everyday clothes they had put on shirts or smocks, so that they appeared dressed in white. Moreover, they had olive garlands on their heads and red crosses each measuring a palm and a half. They were divided into quarters [of the city], according to the custom of the city.

Each quarter had its own standard and chief with the ensign of his quarter. Behind them followed the children, three by three, holding hands. After the four quarters, estimated at six to seven thousand children, there followed under a canopy a panel on which was painted

28. From Piero Parenti, *Storia Fiorentina*, in *Selected Writings of Girolamo Savonarola*, 239–40.

our Lord on the ass, and facing him were the Jews laying down their robes and spreading them before the ass along with olive branches and palms, in accordance with what is reenacted on such a holy Sunday. Also depicted on the said panel was a crown, in accordance with the vision of the aforementioned Fra Girolamo, but before the panel were carried two real crowns dedicated to the King and Queen of life eternal. Behind these followed little girls wearing the same habit. And all were chanting litanies, often crying out: "Long live, long live Christ the King and the Queen of life eternal." Then there followed on a pole the ensign of the *Monte di Pietà*, and [next], according to rank, all the orders of religious and at the end the priests with the bishop. Close behind came all the magistrates of the land, starting with the Colleges, since the Signory remained at the Palace; finally, all the people, men and women, in vast numbers, swelled the crowd.

When the usual routes had been completed, each [group] returned to Santa Maria del Fiore, where a huge altar had been prepared with four containers and ministers. They received all the offerings which were to be used for the foundation of the *Monte di Pietà*. Above the said altar stood the ensign of the Monte, and each one going by it made an offering. Also, through the streets were carried baskets and tubs, in which were collected all the people gave: coins, cloths for a number of purposes, and other things of value, such as embroidered cushions, rings, belts, silver spoons and forks. But because the land was poor and in disarray, it was calculated that the entire sum amounted to about fifteen hundred ducats.

This was the beginning of the *Monte di Pietà*, over which was placed at first a public magistracy of men who would execute this commission, and this subsidy and loan would be supervised from the house of Piero de'Medici, since formerly he had obstructed this laudable work, so that he might get the payback he deserved.

DOCUMENT 29

The Pseudo–Fra Pacifico Burlamacchi on the Burning of the Vanities, February 7, 1497[29]

The Vita di Fra Girolamo Savonarola (The Life of Brother Girolamo Savonarola) *was incorrectly attributed to a Dominican monk originally from Lucca, Pacifico Burlamacchi (1465–1519), a disciple of Savonarola associated with the convent of San Marco, where he fervently protected the friar's memory. The misattribution to Burlamacchi was made by another Dominican follower of Savonarola, Fra Timoteo Bottonio from Perugia. Bottonio sustained the vernacular tradition of* The Life of Savonarola *by adding other miracles and prophecies attributed to Savonarola until the 1560s. This passage describes the Burning of the Vanities.*

Chapter XLb: How He Set Fire to All the Vanities

In the year of the Lord 1498 [actually February 1497], the children, carrying out their duties, began to purge the city anew and found more vain things and of a greater number and beauty, so that as a result, another edifice was built, larger than the previous one, of like model and form, on the top of which was an ancient serpent, and above it presided Lucifer with the seven deadly sins. On the day of Carnival, early in the morning, there was a solemn Communion of men, women, and children—several thousands of them—at the hands of the servant of God; afterward he climbed into the pulpit where he made that protestation . . . as is written. And with great gladness the people went home.

After dinner they arranged a procession prepared by angelic hands. When the people had come to San Marco wearing their proper clothes, with red crosses in their hands, and the children with crowns of flowers on their heads, they went along two by two, according to the order of the quarters of the city, singing litanies and psalms and hymns and sometimes lauds newly composed for the occasion, and after them followed the ensigns of the quarters; that is, the quarter of Santo Spirito

29. From the Pseudo–Fra Pacifico Burlamacchi, *Vita del Beato Hieronimo Savonarola*, in *Selected Writings of Girolamo Savonarola*, 345–48.

had the Virgin with the twelve apostles, upon whom the Holy Spirit descended, an admirably made sculpture, ornately painted, and set on a portable altar with two ornate poles running along each side, under which four youths dressed as angels set their shoulders and so bore it along, and they were all adorned in gold and silk. All these figures were placed in a marvelously constructed tabernacle, and upon them descended a dove representing the Holy Spirit, while the canopy was raised high above the tabernacle, as we said earlier. There were children all dressed alike preceding this mystery, and they sang new lauds, and after [it] the cantors, the guardians with their soldiers, and almoners carried silver vessels to receive alms. After these followed another quarter in the same way with their ensign, St. John the Baptist, figured in a most beautiful tabernacle in high relief, borne in the same way by children and with a canopy, as I said before, according to the order of their quarter. Then followed the quarter of Santa Maria Novella with their emblem of the Virgin ascending into Heaven, also admirably sculpted, and carried in the same way by the children under its canopy. Last of all came the quarter of Santa Croce with its emblem, which was a golden cross rubricated with splendid gems and precious enamels, placed in an ornate tabernacle according to the manner and order of the previous ones, but you should know that in order to distinguish himself, the guardian had his red cross somewhat larger than the others. They were followed by a great multitude of men, and then the girls with the women, and, taking the road by the Via Larga, they entered through the middle door of St. John the Baptist, patron saint of the city of Florence; then, exiting through a side door, they went to the corner of the Carnesecchi and turned round toward the river; after crossing the bridge of Santa Trinità, they turned to the suburb of Santo Iacopo, above the Arno, and came to the Ponte Vecchio, where, crossing the river once again, they came to the gate of Santa Maria. Turning on the Via Vacchereccia, they finally reached the Piazza della Signoria, while all along the way every quarter with its cantors sang so sweetly and pleasantly that it seemed as if Paradise had opened.

When they arrived at the piazza, they found the great edifice better adorned than the previous one; there were some sculpted heads of antique women famous for their beauty, such as the beautiful Bencina, Lena Morella, the beautiful Bina, Maria de'Lenzi, sculpted in expensive marble by famous sculptors, not to mention the other Roman women, such as Lucretia, Faustina, and Cleopatra; there was a Petrarch adorned with illustrations in gold and silver which was worth fifty scudi. To guard this triumph there were soldiers posted at the piazza and servants of the Eight [of Watch and Ward; hence, the police], because, without these guards, many extremely beautiful figures of outstanding craftsmanship and high value would have been stolen. So when the procession reached the piazza, they went all around it; then the quarters positioned themselves according to the order observed in the previous procession and sang songs composed for the occasion of this feast, and after surrounding the edifice and triumph, they blessed it with holy water. The guardians with their lighted torches then came and set fire to it, while the musical instruments of the Signory were sounded along with the trumpets and bells of the palace to give glory, and all the people exulted and sang Te Deum laudamus. When this spectacle had been consumed by the fire in despite of Lucifer and his followers, the procession followed the Via degli Adimari to the Cathedral of Santa Maria del Fiore, and here, praying and singing many lauds, they offered the whole city to God and commended it to the Queen of Florence, presenting to the officers of St. Martin gathered here on that account the coins, which grew and multiplied in greater and greater quantities every year.

Leaving the cathedral, they came along the Via del Cocomero to the Piazza of San Marco. In the middle of this piazza they placed the image of Our Savior triumphant upon the holy Cross together with the four tabernacles and ensigns of the quarters; around these they performed three dances, all the friars in the forefront with great fervor. They removed their hoods as they issued from the convent, and each novice took as a companion one of the children dressed as angels, and [thus] they made the first round; then each of the young friars took one young layman and made the second round, singing; finally, the old friars and priests, setting aside all human wisdom, with olive garlands on their heads, each took an old citizen and made the third dance, enclosing the other two: the first circle was in the middle, the second came after the first, and the third last. They were all exulting and jubilant, singing endless lauds to the image of the Crucifix, and they persevered in this devout fervor till the sun went down, and each went his own way. The servant of God felt such great fervor that he hid himself in a secret place to watch. He was jubilant for very lightness of spirit, and the following morning, while preaching, he greatly commended them, as is written in his sermon; he exhorted the whole city both to be cheered by this great consolation and to take great example [from it]—for all this God be blessed.

Nonetheless, these children suffered so many tribulations and persecutions for wanting to live uprightly and to do good works that many
wondered why such warfare was waged against them by fathers and
mothers, and child-followers of the lukewarm, and the wicked seemingly
of every station; and yet, in spite of so much tribulation and opposition,
they maintained such calm of spirit and peace, such great love and good-
will, such delightful obedience, so much patience and gladness in charity
and joy that everyone was amazed. For, because of the divine grace over-
flowing from their bodies, their faces were bright and shining, so that to
all those who contemplated them, they seemed angels, and the adversar-
ies of truth sometimes became so enraged that, as if instigated by their
leader and guide, Satan, they would begin to throw rocks at these people
and to spit in the faces of the children and on the tabernacles, breaking
the crosses, which they called mandrakes, and throwing them into the
Arno, even going so far as to spit on the beautiful face of our Infant Savior
[Donatello's statue], and they did things which [even] infidels would not
have done, cursing the children and saying many nasty words to them.

Chapter XLI: How a Young Man Who Impeded the Procession Was Punished

But hear the Lord's judgment. When the procession had already passed
the Church of Santa Trinità and the Spini Palace, just at the point
where there is a place which in the vernacular is called *la Pancaccia* [the
Benches], where every day many noble and lazy youths hang around gos-
siping and wasting time, there were many Compagnacci, sons of the devil,
who, carried away by the Furies, began to throw rocks at the back of the
procession in order to confuse them. Suddenly the Spirit of the Lord
came to the children of light and the friends of the truth and of the teaching of the servant of God, who, after removing their robes and making
a shield of them, began to throw the rocks back, and so they began to
prevail against their enemies, who turned tail and were put to flight. Do
not suppose that these were [children] of the vulgar crowd; rather, they
were [the offspring] of the leading men of the city who had been Gon-
faloniers of Justice, Officers of the *Monte* [*Commune*, the public debt],
the Ten of the War Office, and counselors and ambassadors to various
kings and princes and even to the Supreme Pontiff; and, nonetheless, laying aside all dignity and human wisdom, these children fought manfully

against the enemies of Christ. But let us return to the great judgment of God, which was this: a noble youth of the Federighi family, passing by the procession on the bridge at Santa Trinità and passing the children with red crosses in their hands, hurled many insults and then snatched a cross from one of them, snapped it, and threw it in the river. In that very spot after not too many days, the Lord struck him down with the plague called *gavocciolo* [Bubonic plague]. There he was left in his sickness, abandoned by everyone and without the sacraments, and in that very place he died. This was revealed to the whole city and judged to be vengeance taken by God as a punishment.

DOCUMENT 30

Girolamo Benivieni, "Viva nei nostri cuori, o Florentia," A Song about the Graces Promised by God to the City of Florence, Composed for Use in the Prescribed Solemnity and Procession [Palm Sunday], and Sung Publicly on that Occasion in the Year of Our Salvation 1496[30]

Girolamo Benivieni (1453–1542) was a poet and musician, as well as a member of the literary circle around Lorenzo where he met Giovanni Pico della Mirandola, who introduced him to Neoplatonism. By the late 1480s, he—and Pico—had become disciples of Savonarola, and so Benivieni rejected his earlier secular poetry in favor of spiritual verse; and it was Benivieni who in 1496 translated the vernacular sermons and prophecies of Savonarola into Latin. He was an enthusiastic participant in the Burning of the Vanities in February of 1497.

> Long live Christ, your King, O Florence,
> may He live in our hearts; long live the Bride,
> His Daughter and Mother, your Guide and Queen,
> for by Their goodness, by Their clemency,
> you will become richer, more powerful and glorious
> than you ever were. The day draws near,
> nor can such a promise
> or priceless gift prove empty,
> because no human tongue proclaims it,
> but divine goodness.
>
> O you who are fortunate above every city,
> more fortunate, indeed, than anyone would believe
> [possible],

30. From Girolamo Benivieni, "Viva nei nostri cuori, o Florentia," in *Selected Writings of Girolamo Savonarola*, 231–33.

and than even you perhaps think or hope,
although every virtue is dead in you,
and every honor seems to go to whoever has nothing to do
with it [virtue],
yet in you lives that glorious seed
on which our every hope
surely depends, from which must issue the fruit
which through You, O sweet Jesus,
will nourish the whole world with Your true blessings.

Amidst your afflictions, my happy Florence,
you can rightly anticipate your salvation
more than any other [city looks for] joy amidst its greatest
pomps,
for you alone have built your foundations
and your holy gates on the holy mountains.
Your Lord loves [you] more than any other [city].
Of you—oh, [what] immense love—
of you alone are said on earth
things more exalted and glorious
than were ever before seen in you by anyone.

Do you not know that when you were chosen
for such a grace, these words were said in heaven
by your kindly and heavenly Queen?
"O Florence, city beloved by God,
by my Son and by me, keep strong and lively
your faith, prayer and patience,
for by them the power is given
to make you ever blessed in heaven with God
and honored here on earth
among other [cities] like a sun among stars."

Rise, O new Jerusalem, and see,
see your glory. Acknowledge, adore
your Queen and her beloved Son.
In you, city of God, who now sit weeping,
such joy and splendor will yet be born
that not only you but the whole world shall be adorned.

In those happy days
you will see coming to you from the ends [of the earth]
a devout and pilgrim people,
[coming] to the fragrance of your consecrated lily,

Of your noble lily, whose leaves
will extend so far beyond your kingdom
that they will put your ungrateful neighbors in the shade.
Blessed by God are those gathered within you,
and cursed be anyone who has disdain
for your welfare, your glory, and your peace.
You, while it pleases your King,
anticipate that in the blink of an eye,
miraculously,
the veil may be torn which now shadows your glory.

Song, I do not rightly know if perhaps silence might be
more honorable than speech amidst so many doubts,
or if it is advisable for you to show yourself in public.
If the gifts of God were not mentioned in you,
this would be the fault of an ingrate, yet if you speak
or sing of them along with me, they may be ridiculed.
So, then, either you rejoice alone within my breast,
or if you would rather go elsewhere,
never show yourself where
there is no one who at least sees with our eyes.

DOCUMENT 31

Savonarola's Sermon of February 11, 1498, Delivered in Defiance of the Ban on Preaching Issued by Pope Alexander VI in May 1497[31]

Savonarola's relations with the papacy had been strained because of his advice that Florence maintain the French alliance and because his sermons against the corruption of the Church were universally understood to be directed against the Borgia pope, Alexander VI. Savonarola was summoned to Rome in July of 1495, but the friar refused to go. Then in September of 1495 the Church rescinded his license to preach; however, on October 11 he resumed preaching, and in his Lenten sermons of 1496 he attacked the hierarchy of the Church with concentrated venom. In his Lenten sermons the following year Savonarola's rhetoric became even more vituperative, resulting in his excommunication in May 1497. He responded by calling his excommunication without foundation and void, celebrating Mass and taking communion at Christmas. Savonarola's defiance of his excommunication is reflected in this extract from his February 1498 sermon.

Moreover, you say I have preached heretical things. Look a while at what I have written to you and what I have published, see whether these seem like heresies to you. I have tossed you a bone to chew on, as people say. You also say I should stop preaching. I will never do this because it is contrary to all charity. Did you not see that when I stopped preaching there was a drop in righteous living and vices grew and gained courage and everything began to fall into confusion? And so the faith of Christ was laid to the ground and the sheep were left in the hands of the wolves. Look carefully whether you can find any law or any canon or any council that says something contrary to what I have said, and if it does, let it be excommunicated, *and let it be anathema.* If any doctor [of the Church] or bishop says anything contrary to this, let him be called anathema and

---

31. From Girolamo Savonarola, Sermon of February 11, 1498, in *A Guide to Righteous Living and Other Works,* trans. and ed. Konrad Eisenbichler (Toronto: CRRS, 2003), 149–76.

told "You have not studied well." And if there were any pope or anyone else who would speak against what I have said, let him be excommunicated. I am not saying there is any pope who has done so, but if there were any that would do so or say so, I tell you that then this man would not have been the craftsman or the principal agent who moved the saw, but that saw would have been moved by someone else, that is, by the bad influence of other people. I want to assume that his intention was good; if it was bad, let God be the judge of that.

You also say I should comply with this excommunication. I will not comply with it because I do not want to act against charity.

So, this is the reason, according to the super-natural light, as I told you, whereby you can see that an order that goes against charity is not valid. [...]

Now then, Christ, what side do you want to be on? Ours or theirs? You can see that our side has always told the truth and that we have always been immovable and that this doctrine has brought in righteous living and so much fervour and so many prayers, and *yet* we have been excommunicated and they have been blessed. And yet one can see that their doctrine leads to evil deeds, and to giving oneself over to eating and drinking, to avarice, to concubines, to the sale of benefices, and to many lies, and to doing all sorts of wickedness. Which side, then, do you want to be on, Christ? Either on the side of the truth or of lies, on the side of the excommunicated or of the blessed? Christ answers: *ego sum via, veritas et vita* [John 14:6]. Christ says: "I am the truth, and I want to dwell with the side that has truth, and with those whom you say are excommunicated, because they pray and do good deeds, they are united in charity, but these other people are always spreading rumours, they speak all sorts of evil, they are disunited." I say, which side do you want to dwell with, Christ? With the excommunicated or with the blessed? He answers: "These people always sing *Behold, how good and how joyful it is for brothers to live as one*, and they are always joyful; but these other people are always unhappy, their hearts are angry, they have no truth whatsoever. Therefore, I want to dwell with the excommunicated."

The Lord therefore notes that He wants to dwell with the excommunicated and the devil will dwell with the blessed. O, Lord, you have perverted your order; how is your wisdom? You used to want to dwell with the blessed and not with the excommunicated, because to be excommunicated means to be severed and cut off from Christ, and to be given into the hands of the devil, and to go every day from bad to worse. The excommunicated go every day from good to better and they constantly improve. Well, then, you see that the Lord is with us and that He sees that the excommunicated improve daily and become stronger in righteous living, and so He wants to dwell with us.

So, my citizens, you must lay down your life, your wealth, and everything else for the sake of this truth and be ready, like good Christians, to die for love of Christ. Women and children, you must be ready, when necessary, to die for the truth and for love of Christ. My brothers, I want us to lay down even our lives for this truth. My Lord, I turn to you: you died for the truth, and I am happy to die for the truth: I offer myself in sacrifice to you: here I am; I am happy to die for you, and I pray you fervently that I might never die for any other reason but to defend your truth, so that it be the salvation of your chosen ones and of this people. I pray you My Lord, my almighty God, *who are blessed for ever and ever. Amen.*

DOCUMENT 32

The Examination, Execution, and Burning of Savonarola and Two Disciples as Described by Luca Landucci in His Diary[32]

The apothecary diarist Luca Landucci (see p. 101) continued his detailed record of events in Florence with a description of the torture and execution of Savonarola and his two disciples in May of 1498.

19th May. The Pope's envoy and the General of San Marco arrived in Florence, in order to examine Fra Girolamo.

20th May (Sunday). This envoy had him put to the rack, and before he was drawn up he asked him whether the things that he had confessed were true; and the *Frate* replied that they were not, and that he was sent by God. And then they put him on the rack, and he confessed that he was a sinner, the same as he had said before.

22nd May. It was decided that he should be put to death, and that he should be burnt alive. In the evening a scaffold was made, which covered the whole *ringhiera* [the raised platform in front of the Palazzo facing the Piazza] of the *Palagio de' Signori* [Palazzo della Signoria], and then a scaffolding which began at the *ringhiera* next to the "lion" [the marble *marzocco*] and reached into the middle of the Piazza, towards the *Tetto de' Pisani* [La Tettoia dei Pisani was a wooden shed of the fourteenth century opposite the Palazzo della Signoria on the Piazza; it was built by Pisan prisoners of war, hence its name]; and here was erected a solid piece of wood many *braccia* high, and round this a large circular platform. On the aforesaid piece of wood was placed a horizontal one in the shape of a cross; but people noticing it, said: "They are going to crucify him"; and when these murmurs were heard, orders were given to saw off part of the wood, so that it should not look like a cross.

22nd May (Wednesday morning). The sacrifice of the three *Frati* was made. They took them out of the *Palagio* and brought them on to the *ringhiera*, where were assembled the "Eight" and the *Collegi*, the papal envoy,

32. From Luca Landucci, *A Florentine Diary*, 142–43.

the General of the Dominicans, and many canons, priests and monks of divers Orders, and the Bishop of the *Pagagliotti* who was deputed to degrade the three *Frati*; and here on the *ringhiera* the said ceremony was to be performed. They were robed in all their vestments, which were taken off one by one, with the appropriate words for the degradation, it was constantly being affirmed that Fra Girolamo was a heretic and schismatic, and on this account condemned to be burnt; then their faces and hands were shaved, as is customary in this ceremony.

When this was completed, they left the *Frati* in the hands of the "Eight," who immediately made the decision that they should be hanged and burnt; and they were led straight on to the platform at the foot of the cross. The first to be executed was Fra Silvestro, who was hanged to the post and one arm of the cross, and there not being much drop, he suffered for some time, repeating "Jesu" many times whilst he was hanging, for the rope did not draw tight nor run well. The second was Fra Domenico of Pescia, who also kept saying "Jesu"; and the third was the *Frate* called a heretic, who did not speak aloud, but to himself, and so he was hanged. This all happened without a word from one of them, which was considered extraordinary, especially by good and thoughtful people, who were much disappointed, as everyone had been expecting some signs, and desired the glory of God, the beginning of righteous life, the renovation of the Church, and the conversion of unbelievers; hence they were not without bitterness and not one of them made an excuse. Many, in fact, fell from their faith. When all three were hanged, Fra Girolamo being in the middle, facing the *Palagio*, the scaffold was separated from the *ringhiera*, and a fire was made on the circular platform round the cross, upon which gunpowder was put and set alight, so that the said fire burst out with a noise of rockets and cracking. In a few hours they were burnt, their legs and arms gradually dropping off; part of their bodies remaining hanging to the chains, a quantity of stones were thrown to make them fall, as there was a fear of the people getting hold of them; and then the hangman and those whose business it was, hacked down the post and burnt it to the ground, bringing up a lot of brushwood, and stirring the fire up over the dead bodies, so that the very last piece was consumed. Then they fetched carts, and accompanied by the mace-bearers, carried the last bit of dust to the Arno, by the Ponte Vecchio, in order that no remains should be found. Nevertheless, a few good men had so much faith that they gathered the floating ashes together, in fear and secrecy, because it was worth as much as one's life was worth to say a word, so anxious were the authorities to destroy every relic.

SELECT BIBLIOGRAPHY

Acton, Harold. *The Pazzi Conspiracy: The Plot against the Medici.* London: Thames & Hudson, 1979.

Ames-Lewis, Francis, ed. *Cosimo 'il Vecchio' de'Medici, 1389–1464.* Oxford: Clarendon Press, 1992.

Bartlett, Kenneth. *The Civilization of the Italian Renaissance.* Toronto: University of Toronto Press, 2011.

———. *A Short History of the Italian Renaissance.* Toronto: University of Toronto Press, 2013.

Beyer, Andreas, Bruce Boucher, and Francis Ames-Lewis, eds. *Piero de'Medici 'il Gottoso' 1416–1469.* Berlin: Akademie, 1993.

Black, Robert, and John Law, eds. *The Medici: Citizens and Masters.* Villa I Tatti Series, 32. Florence: Villa I Tatti, The Harvard University Center for Italian Renaissance Studies, 2015.

Brown, Alison. *Bartolomeo Scala, 1430–1497, Chancellor of Florence: The Humanist as Bureaucrat.* Princeton, NJ: Princeton University Press, 1979.

———. *Medicean and Savonarolan Florence: The Interplay of Politics, Humanism and Religion.* Turnhout, Belgium: Brepols, 2011.

———. *The Medici in Florence: The Exercise and Language of Power.* Florence: Olschki, 1992.

Brucker, Gene. *The Civic World of Early Renaissance Florence.* Princeton, NJ: Princeton University Press, 1977.

———. *Renaissance Florence.* Berkeley: University of California Press, 1983.

Cohn, Samuel. *Creating the Florentine State: Peasants and Rebellion, 1348–1434.* Cambridge: Cambridge University Press, 1999.

Connell, William, and A. Zorzi, eds. *Florentine Tuscany: Structures and Practices of Power.* Cambridge: Cambridge University Press, 2000.

Crum, Roger, and John Paoletti. *Renaissance Florence: A Social History.* Cambridge: Cambridge University Press, 2006.

Dall'Aglio, Stefano. *Savonarola and Savonarolism.* Toronto: Centre for Reformation and Renaissance Studies, 2010.

De Roover, Raymond. *The Rise and Decline of the Medici Bank, 1397–1494.* Cambridge, MA: Harvard University Press, 1963; reprinted 1999.

Dempsey, Charles. *The Portrayal of Love: Botticelli's Primavera and Humanist Culture at the Time of Lorenzo the Magnificent*. Princeton, NJ: Princeton University Press, 1992.

Field, Arthur. *The Origins of the Platonic Academy of Florence*. Princeton, NJ: Princeton University Press, 1988.

Fletcher, Stella, and C. Shaw, eds. *The World of Savonarola: Italian Elites and Perceptions of Crisis*. Aldershot, UK: Ashgate, 2000.

Fusco, Laurie, and Gino Corti. *Lorenzo de'Medici, Collector and Antiquarian*. Cambridge: Cambridge University Press, 2006.

Garfagnini, Gian Carlo, ed. *Lorenzo il Magnifico e il suo mondo*. Florence: Olschki, 1994.

Goldthwaite, Richard A. *The Building of Renaissance Florence: An Economic and Social History*. Baltimore: Johns Hopkins University Press, 1980.

———. *The Economy of Renaissance Florence*. Baltimore: Johns Hopkins University Press, 2011.

———. *Wealth and the Demand for Art in Italy: 1300–1600*. Baltimore: Johns Hopkins University Press, 1993.

Gombrich, Ernst. "The Early Medici as Patrons of Art." In *Italian Renaissance Studies*, edited by E. F. Jacob. London: Faber & Faber, 1960.

Guicciardini, Francesco. *The History of Italy*, edited and translated by S. Alexander. Princeton, NJ: Princeton University Press, 1984.

Hale, J. R. *The Medici: The Patterns of Control*. London: Thames and Hudson, 1977.

Herzig, Tamar. *Savonarola's Women: Visions and Reform in Renaissance Italy*. Chicago: University of Chicago Press, 2008.

Hibbert, Christopher. *The House of Medici: Its Rise and Fall*. New York: William Morrow, reprinted 1999.

Hook, Judith. *Lorenzo de'Medici: An Historical Biography*. London: Hamish Hamilton, 1984.

Kent, Dale. *Cosimo de'Medici and the Florentine Renaissance: The Patron's Oeuvre*. New Haven, CT: Yale University Press, 2000.

———. *The Rise of the Medici: Faction in Florence, 1426–1434*. Oxford: Oxford University Press, 1978.

Kent, F. W. *Lorenzo de'Medici and the Art of Magnificence*. Baltimore: Johns Hopkins University Press, 2004.

———. *Princely Citizen: Lorenzo de'Medici and Renaissance Florence*. Turnhout, Belgium: Brepols, 2013.

Kohl, Benjamin, and Ronald Witt. *The Earthly Republic: Italian Human-ists on Government and Society*. Philadelphia: University of Pennsylvania Press, 1978.

Macey, Patrick. *Bonfire Songs: Savonarola's Musical Legacy*. Oxford: Clarendon Press, 1998.

Machiavelli, Niccolo. *History of Florence and of the Affairs of Italy: From the Earliest Times to the Death of Lorenzo the Magnificent*, edited by F. Gilbert. New York: Harper Torchbooks, 1960.

Mallett, Michael, and N. Mann, eds. *Lorenzo the Magnificent: Culture and Politics*. London: Warburg Institute, 1996.

Marks, Louis. "The Financial Oligarchy in Florence under Lorenzo." In *Italian Renaissance Studies*, edited by E. F. Jacob. London: Faber & Faber, 1960.

Martines, Lauro. *April Blood: Florence and the Plot against the Medici*. Oxford: Oxford University Press, 2003.

———. *Fire in the City: Savonarola and the Struggle for the Soul of Renaissance Florence*. Oxford: Oxford University Press, 2006.

McGinn, Bernard, ed. *The Compendium of Revelations in Apocalyptic Spirituality: Treatises and Letters of Lactantius, Adso of Montier-en-Der, Joachim of Fiore, the Franciscan Spirituals, Savonarola*. New York: Paulist Press, 1979.

McLean, Paul. *The Art of the Network: Strategic Interaction and Patronage in Renaissance Florence*. Durham: University of North Carolina Press, 2007.

Meltzoff, Stanley. *Botticelli, Signorelli and Savonarola*. Florence: Olschki, 1987.

Najemy, John. *A History of Florence, 1200–1575*. Oxford: Blackwell, 2006.

Parks, Tim. *Medici Money: Banking, Metaphysics, and Art in Fifteenth-Century Florence*. New York: W. W. Norton & Company, 2006.

Pernis, Maria Grazia, and L. S. Adams. *Lucrezia Tornabuoni de'Medici and the Medici Family in the Fifteenth Century*. New York: Lang, 2006.

Phillips, Mark. *The Memoir of Marco Parenti: A Life in Renaissance Florence*. Princeton, NJ: Princeton University Press, 1987.

Polizotto, Lorenzo. *The Elect Nation: The Savonarolan Movement in Florence, 1494–1545*. Oxford: Oxford University Press, 1994.

Ridolfi, Roberto. *The Life of Savonarola*, translated by C. Grayson. London: Routledge & Kegan Paul, 1959.

Rocke, Michael. *Forbidden Friendships: Homosexuality and Male Culture in Renaissance Florence*. Oxford: Oxford University Press, 1996.

Ross, Janet. *The Lives of the Early Medici as Told in Their Correspondence*. London: Chatto & Windus, 1910.

Rubinstein, Nicholas. *The Government of Florence under the Medici, 1434–1494*. Oxford: Oxford University Press, 1966; reprinted 1997.

Savonarola, Girolamo. *Selected Writings of Girolamo Savonarola on Religion and Politics, 1490–1498*, edited and translated by A. Borelli and M. Passaro. New Haven, CT: Yale University Press, 2006.

Steinberg, Ronald. *Fra Girolamo Savonarola, Florentine Art, and Renaissance Historiography*. Athens: Ohio University Press, 1977.

Strathern, Paul. *Death in Florence: The Medici, Savonarola, and the Battle for the Soul of a Renaissance City*. New York: Pegasus Books, 2016.

———. *The Medici: Godfathers of the Renaissance*. New York: Vintage Books, 2009.

Tomas, Natalie. *The Medici Women: Gender and Power in Renaissance Florence*. Aldershot, UK: Ashgate, 2006.

Toscani, Bernard, ed. *Lorenzo de'Medici: New Perspectives*. New York: Lang, 1993.

Unger, Miles. *Magnifico: The Brilliant Life and Violent Times of Lorenzo de'Medici*. New York: Simon & Schuster, reprinted 2009.

Vespasiano da Bisticci. *The Vespasiano Memoirs: Lives of Illustrious Men of the XVth Century*, Renaissance Society of America Reprint Texts 7, translated by William George and Emily Waters, Introduction by Myron P. Gilmore. Toronto: University of Toronto Press in association with the Renaissance Society of America, 1997.

Weinstein, Donald. *Savonarola and Renaissance Florence*. Princeton, NJ: Princeton University Press, 1970.

Weinstein, Donald, and V. Hotchkiss. *Girolamo Savonarola: Piety, Prophecy and Politics in Renaissance Florence*. Dallas: Bridwell, 1994.

GLOSSARY

accoppiatori: Election officials in the Florentine republic. They were responsible for selecting the names of those who were eligible for election to public office. *Accoppiatori* consequently exercised significant influence.

Arrabbiati (**singular** *arrabbiato*)**:** The faction opposed to Savonarola. The term literally means the "angry men."

ars predicandi: The art of preaching. Dominicans in particular prided themselves on their preaching skills. Their designation of O.P. is the Latin abbreviation for Order of Preachers.

Arte del popolo minuto: The Guild of Lesser Citizens. These represented those men in Florence who were common laborers and lesser artisans who had previously been excluded from access to political office. After the Ciompi Revolt such men briefly had their own guild and were consequently eligible for election.

arti maggiori: The seven greater guilds as identified by the Ordinances of Justice. These were judges and notaries, cloth dealers, wool manufacturers, bankers and money-changers, silk merchants, physicians and apothecaries, and furriers.

arti minori: The Fourteen lesser guilds recognized by the Ordinances of Justice. These were butchers, blacksmiths, shoemakers, builders and masons, clothiers, vintners, innkeepers, retailers of provisions, tanners, armorers, ironworkers, saddlers and harness makers, woodworkers, and bakers.

Badia: A monastic institution.

Balia: A temporary committee formed to deal with a particular problem outside the usual structures of government.

Bargello: The palace of the *podestà*, erected in 1250. It also served as a prison and place of execution.

borse: The bags containing the names of eligible guildsmen.

capo (**plural** *capi*): The head of a faction or group in the Florentine republic.

Ciompi: Poor common laborers and lesser artisans with little or no wealth who worked mostly in the textile industry. They had no political rights (except for the brief period following the Ciompi Revolt of 1378), were kept in debt, and often brutally controlled by their employers. Ciompi comprised up to one-quarter of the population of the city, depending on the period and the demand for labor. The origins of the term are obscure.

compagnacci: The gangs of anti-Savonarolan young men who disrupted his sermons and took violent action against the leaders of Savonarola's faction, including the murder of Francesco Valori and his wife just before the friar's arrest. Members of the *compagnacci* came from all classes in society, but were often led by young patricians.

Consiglio dei Cento: The Council of One Hundred. In August of 1458, Cosimo de'Medici and his faction neutralized his opponents through the creation of a new, powerful Council of One Hundred with members consisting of loyal Medici supporters. The Council chose important officials and defined the legislation that was to be debated in the other, older republican councils.

consorteria (**plural** *consorterie*): An alliance or association of powerful families to protect their interests. These alliances were often reinforced by marriage, neighborhood, or economic ties.

Consulte e Pratiche: These were debates and discussions held at the discretion of the Signoria to determine the opinions of powerful Florentines, both within and outside the government. Important magistrates and influential citizens, respected for their wealth, experience, and knowledge, would be summoned to discuss pressing issues. *Consulte e Pratiche* were an effective way of gauging elite opinion on important issues and could serve to widen public debate beyond those men holding public office.

contado: The rural territory surrounding and usually dependent upon the city of Florence.

damnatio memoriae: A condemnation of a person's place in the collective memory of a state, and a conscious erasure of the name and memory of an individual declared an enemy of the people.

divieto: That law that excluded several members of a family from holding high office simultaneously.

estimo: A direct wealth tax, based on an assessment of an individual's total net worth. It was extremely unpopular among the elite, leading to its abolition in 1315, although it was temporarily revived under Charles of Calabria in 1326.

florin: A gold coin introduced by Florence in 1252. It was carefully shielded from devaluation and became the international currency for banking and trade.

Fraticelli: Literally, "Little Brothers." The term refers to the strictest sect of the Spiritual Franciscans, those followers of Francis of Assisi who adhered rigorously to his vows of poverty. They opposed the wealth of the Church and consequently were declared heretical in 1296. They continued, however, to teach an almost mystical social gospel among the poor.

Ghibellines: Individuals, families, factions, or cities that recognized the authority of the Holy Roman Emperor as the source of secular sovereignty. The term derives from the name of the German castle of Waiblingen, a stronghold of the Hohenstaufen emperors and hence their battle cry; Ghibelline is the Italians pronunciation.

gonfaloniere della giustizia: The standard bearer of justice, the most prestigious of the nine priors who formed the collective executive in the Florentine republic. The position was created by the Ordinances of Justice in 1293 and carried with it responsibility for their enforcement. For the two months he held office, the *gonfaloniere* also had possession of the ceremonial standard of the republic.

governo largo: Literally, "broad government." The term refers to a regime that afforded political eligibility to as many men as possible.

governo stretto: Literally, "narrow government." The term indicates a regime dedicated to restricting eligibility for elected office to as few men as possible, usually the elite of the city.

grandi: Urban, often mercantile families that acquired great wealth early in the history of the city and became associated through marriage or style of life with the *magnati* (or landed magnates). These families suffered the loss of power with the magnates under the Ordinances of Justice.

Guelfs: Individuals, families, factions, or cities that recognized the authority of the pope as the source of secular sovereignty. The term derives again from a German word, *Welf*, the family name of the dukes of Bavaria. It, too, became a war cry as early as 1140.

Il Gottoso: The Gouty, a description of Piero di Cosimo de'Medici who suffered terribly from gout. The term, however, seems to have been used only after his death.

Il Magnifico: Literally, "The Magnificent." This description of Lorenzo de'Medici was not uncommon for remarkable men and hence not specific to him.

Il Poverello: The little poor one. A popular name for St. Francis of Assisi.

Lucchesi: The people of the Tuscan city of Lucca.

Maggior Consiglio: The Great Council of the Venetian Republic. It consisted of the sane, adult males from every patrician family and was the source of sovereignty in the republic. It was closed to new members (although not completely) by the *Serrata* (Closure) of 1297. Later, entry was restricted to those names inscribed in the Golden Book, the official state patrician genealogy of Venice.

magnati: Landed, often feudal magnates who controlled vast rural estates in Tuscany as well as fortified palaces in the city of Florence. They were sometimes descended from Germanic knights as well as Italian feudal clans.

Monte: The consolidated debt of the commune of Florence established in 1343. Shares were sold in this "Mountain" of state financial obligations to service the debt.

Monte di Pietà: A religious lending institution, often involving pawnbroking, which operated like a charity by giving small loans to the poor at much lower rates of interest (or none).

Museo degli Argenti: Located on the ground floor of Palazzo Pitti from 1861, the Silver Museum, displays gems, cameos, semiprecious stones, ivory, jewels, and silver, including the collection of Lorenzo de' Medici.

novi cives: Latin for "New Citizens." These were men from families only recently enriched and often only recently matriculated into a guild or even relatively new to Florence. In general, this group sponsored a more open government in opposition to old, established, patrician clans and emphasized the integrity of the republic rather than special interests.

Palazzo della Signoria or Palazzo Vecchio: The town hall of Florence, designed by Arnolfo di Cambio, and begun in 1299. It was built by the commune after the Ordinances of Justice to provide a place for the elected magistrates of the city and their staff to work and live. Priors had to live in the palace during their two months' tenure of office. Officially named the palace of the Signoria, it became the Old Palace (Palazzo Vecchio) when Grand Duke Cosimo I moved his family to the Palazzo Pitti, the "new" palace.

palle: Literally "balls," that is, the symbols on the Medici coat of arms, and hence the rallying cry of their faction.

Palleschi: Medici supporters, so named from the *palle* or balls on the family's coat of arms.

Parlamento: Summoned by the ringing of the great bell in the tower of the Palazzo della Signoria, adult male citizens of the city assembled in the Piazza della Signoria to approve or reject important decisions, establish special committees for particular purposes (*Balìe*), or participate in extraordinary events. This was an assembly representing the direct sovereignty of the citizens, although it was occasionally compromised by intimidation or controlled information.

Pater Patriae: Latin for "Father of the Nation." It was an honor reserved for the greatest statesmen and patriots in ancient Rome, bestowed upon figures such as Camillus, Caesar, and Cicero. It was awarded to Cosimo de' Medici, Il Vecchio, at the end of his life.

Piagnoni (singular Piagnone): The faction in support of Savonarola. It was originally a derogatory term, meaning "snivellers" or "weepers," as many of the monk's adherents would cry during his sermons.

podestà: From 1180, the head of Florence's security forces and a kind of chief magistrate. He was always a foreigner and held office for only one year to prevent the subversion of the commune. If his administration had been successful and his accounts reconciled, the *podestà* was permitted to display his coat of arms in the courtyard of the Bargello.

Popolo e Libertà: Liberty and the People. The rallying cry of those opposed to the Medici.

quartieri: Florence was divided into four quarters (*quartieri*), each of which sent neighborhood representatives to the various organs of the republic. The neighborhoods were also the center of militia activity and played a very important role in determining slates of eligible candidates for election to office.

regno: The kingdom, as Naples was usually called, because it was the only kingdom on the Italian peninsula.

Sfortunato: Piero the Unlucky was the descriptive name given to Piero di Lorenzo de'Medici, who was expelled from the city in 1494. It was applied mostly after his death, which occurred by drowning in a river near Gaeta while retreating with the French army in 1503.

signori (singular signore): Italian for "Lords." This is a general term for despotic rulers in Renaissance Italy, as well as just being a polite term of address.

Signoria: The collective term for the senior magistrates of the republic after 1293, especially the nine priors (*priori*).

Stanze per la Giostra di Giuliano de'Medici: *Stanzas for the Tournament of Giuliano de'Medici* is an unfinished poem by Angelo Poliziano begun in 1475 to celebrate the tournament held on January 29 of that year in Piazza Santa Croce. The poem was never finished because Giuliano de'Medici was murdered in 1478 during the Pazzi Conspiracy.